POISONOUS INSECTS - AN OVERVIEW

K THIRUVENGADAM

Made with ♥ on the Notion Press Platform
www.notionpress.com

Dedicated to all entomologist...

Contents

Prologue

As a human being, all of us are having fear to touch, handle, bite and even to be near to insects. So the author brings the knowledge about poisonous insects to readers.

Lets reduce readers fear on insects by every pages with joy.

CHAPTER ONE

Introduction

1.0.Introduction :

Only a few of the very large number of wasp species in a social life; these species are referred to as social wasps. Some social wasps are predators for most or all of the year and provide a great benefit by killing large numbers of plant-feeding insects and nuisance flies; others are exclusively scavengers. Wasps become a problem only when they threaten to sting humans. One of the most troublesome of the social wasps is the yellowjacket. Yellowjackets, especially ground- and cavity-nesting ones such as the western yellowjacket tend to defend their nests vigorously when disturbed. Defensive behavior increases as the season progresses and colony populations become larger while food becomes scarcer. In fall, foraging yellowjackets are primarily scavengers and they start to show up at picnics, barbecues, around garbage cans, at dishes of dog or cat food placed outside, and where ripe or overripe fruit are accessible. At certain times and places, the number of scavenger wasps can be quite large.(Akre *et.al.*, 1981).

Hymenopterous insects (ants, wasps, bees, hornets and yellow jackets) cause more severe allergic reactions than do other insects. However, spiders such as the brown recluse and the black widow are also poisonous. The nettling caterpillars such as the larvae of the saddleback moth, io moth, the hag moth, and the flannel moth can inflict a painful reaction upon contact. Hypersensitive individuals may experience swelling, nausea, and generalized systemic reactions. Ants, particularly the imported fire ant, can inflict a painful sting that will result in a pustule at the sting site. (Ledbetter,1985)

Insects not only act as pests of human property but also lead fatal problems to humans by transmitting certain diseases and causing direct poisoning. In USA, on the basis of death certificates more humans are died due to insect poisoning than to snake venoms. Two to three million people in the United States are severely allergic to the venom of stinging insects (Strother, 1985).

The major poisonous insects are identified in the order Hymenoptera, followed by Lepidoptera, Hemiptera, Diptera, Coleoptera, Blattodea, Siphonaptera, Phthiraptera. The most venomous non-insect order is Araneae, followed by the order Sarcoptiformes. (Ledbetter,1985).

Common reactions to toxic substances are pain, itching, swelling or other symptoms. In addition to the effects of the venom itself, some people have allergic reactions that can be serious. Symptoms of allergic reactions include difficulty breathing or swallowing, weakness, dizziness, vomiting, rashes or unconciousness. If the victim has any of these symptoms, seek medical help quickly. Each year in the U.S. about 25 deaths are reported from bee and wasp stings, five from spider bites and scorpion stings, and 15 from snake bites.(Brodie, 1989)(Dress *et.al.*, 1998)

The stingers remain adhered to the skin and if the venom gland is pressed, more content is inoculated. Careful removal of the remaining stingers modifies the prognosis of the victim of envenomation. The treatment of one to a few bee or wasp stings can consist of antihistamines and topical corticosteroids, but severe toxicity will require symptomatic treatment because there is no antivenom for bee stings. Appropriate emergency room treatment includes systemic corticosteroids, antihistamines, and millesimal adrenaline owing to the high risk of death.(Cardoso, 2009)

Over 95 percent of these are completely harmless, less than 1 percent of the rest go out of their way to torment people. Insects and other invertebrates attack people for two reasons to obtain food or to defend themselves. Blackflies, ticks, mosquitoes, chiggers, deer flies and horse flies require animals or human blood as food. Females use the protein from blood to make eggs. Any other bite or sing is a defensive or protective reaction by the insects. Many insects feed on each other or similar small creature. (Craven *et.al.*, 2010)

Most insect stings are associated with transient local reactions characterized by pain, swelling, and redness, which usually last from a few hours to a few days and generally resolve with simple treatment measures. More extensive local reactions are usually IgE mediated and cause swelling extending from the sting site, peaking in 24 to 48 hours, and lasting 1 week or more. The frequency of large local reactions is estimated at 5% to 15% but is uncertain because of the variable definition of large local reactions (ranging from 5-8 cm to 4-6 inches in diameter). After insect stings, systemic reactions that are potentially life-threatening occur in 0.4% to 0.8% of children and up to 3% of adults. A review of national mortality data in the United States from 1980 to 1999 found that at least 40 deaths per year are a result of sting induced anaphylaxis, with the likelihood of additional sting related deaths in persons reported to have died of cardiovascular causes or "unknown cause." These numbers might be understated based on International Classification of Diseases–ninth revision coding in emergency departments. The diagnosis of stinging insect hypersensitivity should be confirmed after a systemic reaction, and it is imperative that appropriate treatment be instituted to prevent serious reactions from subsequent stings, including a prescription for and instructions on how to use self administered epinephrine. Prompt recognition and treatment of systemic reactions and appropriate allergy management, as described in this practice parameter, can reduce the occurrence of future systemic reactions and fatalities. This parameter addresses the management of allergic reactions from yellow jacket, hornet, wasp, honeybee, and imported fire ant stings. Much less is known about allergic reactions to stings of other insects, and they are not the subject of this parameter. It should be noted that with respect to diagnosis and treatment, the use of the terms venom immunotherapy, VIT, venom testing.(David *et.al*, 2010)

In India, no records are available on insect poisoning and death occurred. Therefore, present study is aimed to report the diversity of poisonous insects with respect to their identifying features, life cycle pattern, source and nature of poison and control including treatment to poisoning. (Sathe, 2014).

Venomous animals pose a significant health risk in most places of the world, particularly in Africa, Southeast Asia, and Tropical America, where epidemiologic studies on these animals are limited to snake bites and scorpion stings. Little information is known about the remaining venomous animals. Although severe reactions may be seen following bee stings and other insect bites, we do not have sufficient information about their effects. These reactions may be local or systemic. Local reactions are often characterized by pain, swelling, erythema, itching, and blister, and overall, type 1 mast cells surround the sting site and mediate an anaphylactic reaction. Toxication due to honey bee or wasp varies in their clinical manifestations. Most people often present with local allergic reactions including pain, redness, and swelling at the site of sting, which generally fades in a couple of hours. However, signs in severe cases may include myocardial infarction, pulmonary edema, bleeding, kidney failure, and life threatening anaphylactic shock. Neurologic symptoms have scarcely been reported in the literature but include encephalitis, acute disseminated encephalomyelitis, extrapyramidal clinical signs, and polyneuritis.(Yurtseven *et.al.*, 2014)

Arthropods belong to the invertebrate Phylum Arthropoda. The name arthropod comes from the Greek *arthron* meaning joint and *pod*, meaning foot, which is one of their characteristic features. They also have an external *skeleton*, or exoskeleton, made of chitin. The Arthropoda phylum contains the most species on Earth, mainly due the number of animals in the Insecta Class.Arthropod species use toxins for defense and to kill prey. Some individuals are poisonous (e.g., certain beetles release toxins when pressed or crushed), whereas others inject venom using an apparatus, which can cause systemic repercussions in the prey, as observed with the stings of certain spiders and scorpions.(Haddad, 2015).

Systemic allergic reactions to insect stings affect up to 5% of the population during their lifetime, and up to 32% of beekeepers. Such reactions can be fatal, albeit very rarely, and fear of a further systemic reaction (SR) can lead to significant anxiety and quality of life impairment. A recent Cochrane systematic review confirmed that venom immunotherapy (VIT) is an effective treatment for people who have had a systemic allergic reaction to an insect sting. VIT reduces risk of a further SR (relative risk 0.10, 95% confidence interval 0.03–0.28), but VIT also reduces risk of a future large local reaction, and significantly improves disease-specific quality of life.

However, health economic analysis showed that VIT is generally not cost effective for preventing future SRs; most people are stung infrequently, most SRs resolve without long-term consequences, and a fatal outcome is extremely rare. VIT only becomes cost effective if one is stung frequently (eg, beekeepers) or if quality of life improvement is considered. Thus, for most people with insect sting allergy, anxiety and quality of life impairment should be the overriding consideration when making treatment decisions, highlighting the importance of a patient-centered approach. Areas which need to be explored in future research include efforts to improve the safety and convenience of VIT such as the use of sublingual immunotherapy; quality of life effects of venom allergy in children and adolescents as well as their parents; and the optimal duration of treatment.(Ludman *et.al.*, 2015)

The groups of arthopods discussed include the class Arachnida (spiders and scorpions, which are responsible for many injuries reported worldwide, including Brazil); the subphylum Myriapoda, with the classes Chilopoda and Diplopoda (centipedes and millipedes); and the subphylum Hexapoda, with the class Insecta and the orders Coleoptera (beetles), Hemiptera (stink bugs, giant water bugs, and cicadas), Hymenoptera (ants, wasps, and bees), and Lepidoptera (butterflies and moths).(Haddad, 2015)

The identified poisonous insects families are vespidae, apidae, formicidae, ampulicidae, cimicidae, reduvidae, pentatomidae, belastomatidae, syntomidae, erebidae, limacodidae, limantriidae, saturnidae, megalopygidae, meloidae, staphylinidae, blattidae, culicidae, tabanidae, oestridae, simuliidae, glossinidae, pulicidae and polyplacidae. The non- insect families are theridiidae, sicariidae, eutichuridae, ctenidae, hexathelidae and sarcoptidae, which are the highly poisonous in nature.

CHAPTER TWO

Impact of poisonous insects

2.0. Impact of poisonous insects :

Reactions to insect stings may be immediate (within two hours) or delayed (after two hours). The most common type is the immediate local reaction. This consists of immediate pain, swelling, and redness and is considered a normal reaction. Although annoying to the individual, it is not considered a serious reaction. Occasionally, a local reaction may become very large (for example, involving the entire arm). This is also not considered serious unless the reaction occurs on head, face, or neck. In that case, a physician should be consulted. When the insect sting produces reactions which are remote from the site of the sting, a systemic or anaphylactic reaction has occurred. This happens in a few sensitive individuals and consists of swelling of the eyes and lips, hives breaking out on the body, tightness in the chest, faintness, and difficulty breathing. If any combination of these symptoms occurs, a physician should be seen immediately. A similar reaction may occur in an individual that is not sensitive if he or she receives a large number of stings. This is considered a toxic reaction. Again, a physician should be consulted. (Ledbetter, 1985)

Systemic anaphylaxis following Hymenoptera insect sting has been widely studied. Prevalence rates in the general population vary from region to region,1 generally ranging from 0.15% to 4%.2"9 In the largest study of an unselected group of 2,067 adults aged 20-60 years, 1.2% of the subjects had a history of systemic anaphylaxis. Health status has long been recognized as an important factor in occupational function. Specifically, allergic sting reactions have been investigated in selected occupational groups. Terr reports that atopic bee-keepers are at high risk of sting anaphylaxis owing to their sensitdzation by inhalation of dried bee venom allergen during the course of occupational exposure to a large number of insect stings. The same author found that almost 50% of all beekeepers and their families had a history of generalized reactions to bee sting. In another study, 3.3% of the beekeepers examined had systemic reactions to bee venom. Systemic anaphylactic reaction is an acute, potentially life-threatening episode which in addition to its physical effect may precipitate apprehension and anxiety. Upon recovery, the traumatic event and the fear of a subsequent life-threatening episode may affect social and occupational behaviour of the affected individuals. In this group, we have demonstrated like others before that exposure to contact with the stinging insect determines the risk for an anaphylactic reaction. Therefore, reason and fear dictate avoiding situations that increase exposure to insects such as outdoor activities. Employment is included in the list of the Word Health Organization's 'Health for the Year 2000' plans; recent legislation has also been targeted at improving the occupational status of people with various disabilities. However, insect venom allergy, in relation to employment, has not received direct attention. This cross-sectional study was conducted to evaluate the impact of a prior reaction to insect sting of the Hymenoptera order on the occupational activities of patients undergoing insect venom immunotherapy.(Kahan *et.al.*, 1997)

Insect bites or stings may lead to mild irritation, itching, redness and swelling and may often go away within a few hours. In some cases however there may be complications after being bitten or stung by the insect. 1-5 Common complications include allergic reactions, secondary infections and so forth.

2.1. Allergic reactions to insect bites :

Allergic reactions like rashes, hives, nettle rash, facila swelling (angioedema) may be seen. Severe allergic reactions or anaphylactic shock may be potentially life threatening. Symptoms include breathing problems, rapid fall in blood pressure, shock, swelling and constriction of the air passages, swelling of the face, lips and neck etc.(Garbutt *et.al.*,2013)

2.1.1. Secondary infections :

Insect bites or stings may often be itchy and repeated scratching may lead to skin abrasions and predispose to skin infections. Some of the skin infections may manifest as sores and blisters that are often filled with pus. This is called impetigo. An inflammation and pus point may often affect hair follicles of the skin and lead to folliculitis. When large areas of skin and underlying tissues are affected, it is called cellulitis.if the infection spreads to the lymph nodes of the armpits, groin or neck, it is termed lymhangitis. While folliculitis and impetigo may be treated with locally applied antibiotic creams and ointments, more generalized infections like cellulitis or lymphangitis may require oral antibiotic pills.(Garbutt *et.al.*,2013) (Abrishami, 1971)

Lyme disease :

This is borne by a species of tick known as *Ixodes ricinus*. There are around a thousand new cases of this disease in England and Wales every year. There may be a red rash at the site of the bite that spreads gradually.Antibiotics are usually used to treat the infection. If left untreated Lyme disease may affect the central nervous system and lead to complications like facial weakness or paralysis, meningitis or encephalitis. Lyme disease over long term may also lead to joint problems like arthritis and heart muscle problems like myocarditis. The tissue layer that cover the heart called the pericardium may also be inflamed (pericarditis) with Lyme disease.(Garbutt *et.al.*,2013)

West Nile virus infection :

This virus is carried by mosquitoes. Usually there are influenza like symptoms of fever, headache, body aches, nausea, vomiting, and sometimes swollen lymph nodes or a skin rash. Complications include encephalitis and meningitis and may manifest with seizures.

Malaria :

Malaria is a parasitic infection that is carried by mosquitoes. It is common in hot and humid climates. Travellers to tropical countries often bring back the infection to more developed and cooler countries. Malaria is manifested with fever, chills and rigor and may lead to severe complications and even death without treatment. There are two main types of malaria infection with *Plasmodium vivax* and *Plasmodium falciparum*. Infection with *P. Falciparum* is potentially life threatening if not detected and treated early.

Rocky Mountain Spotted Fever :

Rocky Mountain Spotted Fever is caused by bacterium *Rickettsia rickettsii* that is transmitted by infected ixodid (hard) ticks. There are three main symptoms of fever, rash, and history of tick bite. There may be nausea, vomiting, severe headache, and loss of appetite, pain in the abdomen, muscle aches and diarrhoea. After initial 2 to 5 days there may be a red rash on the wrists, forearms, palms, soles and ankles.(Garbutt *et.al.*,2013)

2.1.2. Other insect borne diseases:

Other insect borne diseases include:

- Relapsing fever and Chagas disease transmitted by bed bugs in Mexico
- Yellow fever transmitted by mosquitoes
- Dengue fever transmitted by mosquitoes
- Onchocerciasis by black flies
- Trypanosomiasis by tsetse flies or by reduvid bugs
- Leishmaniasis transmitted by sandflies
- Loiasis by Deer flies or Mango flies
- Ross River fever by mosquitoes (Garbutt *et.al.*,2013)

2.2. Impact of poisonous insects on humans :

Insect sting reactions can be classified as immediate or delayed based upon their timing. Reactions can also be toxic, or allergic. A toxic reaction is due to poisons in the venom itself acting on cells and tissues of the body. Whereas, a true allergic response is a result of the immune system making specific allergic antibodies (IgE) to compounds of the insect venom, leading with exposure to the generation and release of a variety of chemicals such as histamine that act on surrounding tissue to cause the symptoms associated with allergic reactions. (National Jewish Health, 2005 & 2009)

2.2.1.Immediate Reactions

Immediate reactions are those reactions occurring within four hours of a sting and can be further divided into local, large local, anaphylactic and toxic reactions.

2.2.1.1.Local Reactions

Immediate local reactions are often considered the "normal reaction". Signs and symptoms may consist of:

- Pain
- Redness
- Swelling
- Mild itching that lasts for several hours

Signs and symptoms of immediate localized reactions are limited to the area of the sting site. Local reactions can occur in individuals who are not insect allergic.

2.2.1.2.Toxic Reactions

In the event of a sting from a poisonous spider or insect; or multiple, simultaneous stings from otherwise non-poisonous insects (as might be the case when a nest is disturbed, or when Africanized honeybees are involved); a toxic reaction may result. Toxic reactions are not caused by an allergic response, but by poisons in the venom that acts as a poison. Local and toxic reactions can be seen in individuals who are not insect sting allergic, although some patients who experience toxic reactions can become allergic to insect venom later. Symptoms of a toxic reaction vary depending on the toxicity of the venom of the insect or spider, the individual's tolerance for that particular venom, and the amount of venom injected.

Common Signs and Symptoms of Toxic Reactions to Insect Venom:

- Rapid swelling at the site of the sting
- Headache
- Weakness
- Light headedness
- Drowsiness
- Fever
- Diarrhea
- Muscle spasms
- Fainting (syncope)
- Seizures

Usually, symptoms lessen or go away within 48 hours. Hives and shortness of breath may occur in an allergic reaction, but not in a toxic reaction, although it is possible to have both a toxic reaction and an allergic reaction at the same time. A toxic reaction can be life-threatening and may lead to heart problems, shock, and death. If a toxic reaction is suspected, or seek professional medical attention immediately. (National Jewish Health, 2005 & 2009)

2.2.1.3. Large Local Reactions

Large local reactions are characterized by redness and swelling that extends from the sting site over a large surrounding area. These reactions often peak within 48 to 72 hours and last up to 10 days. They may be accompanied by fatigue, low-grade fever, mild nausea and malaise and are often misdiagnosed as cellulitis.

2.2.1.4. Anaphylaxis

Anaphylaxis is the most severe insect sting reaction. This is an allergic reaction, involving multiple organ systems at the same time, most often begins within minutes of the sting although it can occasionally begin an hour or so later.

Common Signs and Symptoms of Anaphylaxis May Include:

- Flushing, itching

- Hives
- Sneezing, runny nose
- Nausea, vomiting, diarrhea
- Abdominal cramping
- Heart irregularities
- Swelling in the throat
- Severe trouble breathing
- Loss of blood pressure (hypotension)
- Loss of consciousness
- Shock

2.2.2.Delayed Reactions

Reactions occurring more than 4 hours after a sting are classified as delayed reactions. There have been isolated reports of serum sickness-like syndromes occurring about a week after a sting. Other unusual reactions that have been reported in association with insect stings include Guillain-Barre syndrome, glomerulonephritis, myocarditis, vasculitis and encephalitis.

Common Signs and Symptoms of Delayed Allergic Reactions to Insect Stings :

- Hives
- Fever
- Malaise
- Joint pain
- Pain or partial paralysis of extremities (hands, arms, feet, and legs)
- Kidney pain
- Chest pain (angina)
- Swelling
- Headache, dizziness, loss of consciousness

These patients are at risk for anaphylaxis to subsequent stings and are candidates for venom immunotherapy. (National Jewish Health, 2005 & 2009)

2.3. Impact of poisonous insects on animals :

Dogs are playful animals and are often found sniffing and exploring unusual places. They tend to sniff under the trash bins, below the ledges and mysterious corners of porches and sheds and love digging up the soil. These places are home to a number of insects which will not hesitate to bite the unsuspecting, curious pooch. At one time or another, this adventurous behavior will lead to insect bites on your dog. Although, you may think of it as a minor insect bite, many insect bites on dogs lead to numerous reactions and dog allergies. It is important to recognize and understand the types of bites and their possible (Pet Assure Corp, 2017)

Symptoms :

Insect bites on dogs are usually due to the sting of bees, wasps, hornets or ants. If your dog is bitten by any of these insects, he may show symptoms within 20 minutes of the bite. You should keep a close watch on your dog as mild symptoms develop after 12 - 24 hours.

If you observe insect bites on a dog's belly, it means that the dog has been bitten by either wasps or ants. Bees also sting on the hairless areas of the dog. The most common place to observe insect bites on dogs is on the face, head or areas around the mouth. Stings and insect bites on dogs results in inflammation and pain. This may take about an hour to subside. In cases where the dog is bitten by honey bees or wasps, there will be redness and the sting site will feel hot to the touch. If the stinger is left behind, it contains muscle tissues that keep contracting and injecting more venom into the dog.

The best way to remove the stinger is scrapping it off using a credit card or a similar object. Do not use a tweezersto pull out the stinger as it may cause the stinger to release more venom. You may also find flea or tick bites on your dog. When the dog is bitten by a flea, it is generally not one flea, but a number fleas that have made their home in your dog's fur coat. If your dog scratches and bites the various parts of his body repeatedly, it means he is infested with fleas. Ticks are also common pests that can cause serious bites on dogs. These tiny pests attach themselves to the dog's skin and suck blood till they are full. Once full, they drop off and die. Even though the tick dies, this bite can lead to many deadly diseases in both dogs and even the dog owner. Dogs can also be bitten by spiders.

There are many poisonous spiders. Spider venom can cause a reaction the minute it comes in contact with the dog's skin. Most of the spiders cannot penetrate their fangs into the dog skin and do not pose much of a threat. However, black widows spiders can penetrate the skin and cause serious consequences. (Pet Assure Corp, 2017)

2.3.1. Symptoms of Insect bites on animals can include the following reactions:

- Swelling on the eyelids
- Swelling on ear flaps
- Swelling on the lips and in some cases the entire face. In this case, it is known as *angiedema.*
- If the dog is bitten on the nose or mouth, it will lead to large swelling and the animal will have difficulty breathing, Urticaria, also known as "hives" which displays as welts are observed on the skin. These bites are usually itchy and can cause anaphylactic reactions.
- Wheezing
- Weakness
- Unconsciousness
- Weak pulse
- Increased heart rate and fever which may cause the animal to go into shock.
- Other symptoms of insect bites on dogs may lead to cold extremities, trembling, vomiting, diarrhea and collapse.

Treatment :

- Apply aloe vera gel on the site of infection
- For bumps and sores, you can try gently applying a paste of baking soda and water several times a day till the bumps recede.
- For irritation, try applying milk of magnesia, calamine lotion or hydrocortisone cream several times a day to ease the irritation. You can also apply regular oatmeal or colloidal oatmeal on the bite site to help relieve the irritation.
- Once the stinger gone, bathe the area with a diluted solution of baking soda mixed with water. Prepare the solution by adding one part baking soda to several parts water. Apply a cold pack for several minutes to help reduce the swelling and pain. Repeat the cold pack several times a day.
- You can mix 1 teaspoon of Epsom salt in 2 cups warm water and boil it. Keep it in the refrigerator to maintain its freshness. Bathe the dog with this mixture, to treat irritated and itchy paws and skin. To treat hot spots on skin, saturate a cotton ball with witch hazel and apply it to the spot for several days.(Pet Assure Corp, 2017)

2.4. Impact of poisonous insects as parasitic in nature :

Three types of lice are so well adapted to life with man that they normally are unable to survive on another host. Two of these are full-time residents on man's body. The other lives in man's clothing and is entirely dependent upon him for food, temperature and humidity. These parasitic insects are head louse, human body louse, fleas, which is harmful to humans and other insects having relative parasitic characters are bed bug, kissing bug, blood sucking or biting flies(mosqutoes blackflies, punkies, horse fly, stable fly, horn fly and snipe fly) and these cause myiasis .(Lawson *et.al.*,1996)

Myiasis:

Myiasis is defined as any disease that results from the infestation of tissues or cavities of the body by larvae of flies. Most often the larval forms are the maggots of blow flies, house flies, flesh flies, screwworm flies, lesser house flies, or bottle flies. The larvae of bot flies and warble flies also attack man.

1. Obligate myiasis: Obligate myiasis of man occurs when the human bot fly attacks people. This is found mainly in the southern U.S. and Mexico. Eggs are deposited on the skin by the female fly or they may be carried to the human by a female mosquito. Larvae bore into the skin soon after hatching and settle down to feeding in one location. Full grown larvae cause lesions in the skin. They leave through an opening in the skin and drop to the ground to complete their life cycle.
2. Accidental myiasis: This is a general term which includes all the other fly larvae which invade humans. Certain species are obligate parasites of horses, cattle, sheep, or rodents but on rare occasions have been known to attack man. Most cases of maggot myiasis in man are attributable to species which ordinarily develop in some form of decaying organic matter. (Lawson *et.al.*,1996)

2.5. Impact of poisonous insects as predacious in nature :

The term parasitoid wasp refers to a large evolutionary grade of hymenopteran superfamilies, mainly in the Apocrita. The parasitic or parasitoid Apocrita are divided into some dozens of families. They are parasitoids of various animals, mainly other arthropods .Many of them are considered beneficial to humans because they control populations of agricultural pests. A few are unwelcome because they attack other benefical insects. Parasitoid wasps are considered beneficial as they control the population of many pest insects. They are increasingly being released directly into regions specifically for the use of biological pest control "A number of parasitic wasp species are commercially available from insectaries and are purchased and released in augmentative biological control programs. Other species have been imported from other countries from which pests have been accidentally introduced without their natural enemies and released to reintroduce the natural enemy with its host, a practice called importation, or "classical" biological control and which occasionally results in sustained suppression (Dress *et.al.*, 1999)

Such predators have powerful enzymes and protein in their saliva that paralyze, kill, or digest their prey. If one of these predacious creature is mishandled, it can inflict a painful bite that may take time to heal. Although the bite may be mistaken for a sting, there is no stinger left behind. The only treatment required is to put ice on the site if swelling develops. Some type of hairy or spiny caterpillars are covered with “urticating” or stinging hairs. These hairs contain a poison cell gland and if rubbed, the hair will break, releasing enzymes that cause blisters, burns or rashes. (Craven *et.al.*, 2010)

Direct Injection of Venom by a Predatory Wasp into Cockroach Brain :

Here,use direct evidence for injection of venom by a wasp into the central nervous system of its cockroach prey. Venomous predators use neurotoxins that generally act at the neuromuscular

junction, resulting in different types of prey paralysis. The sting of the parasitoid wasp *Ampulex compressa* is unusual, as it induces grooming behavior, followed by a long-term lethargic state of its insect prey, thus ultimately providing a living meal for the newborn wasp larvae.

These behavioral modifications are induced only when a sting is inflicted into the head. These unique effects of the wasp venom on prey behavior suggest that the venom targets the insect’s central nervous system. The mechanism by which behavior modifying compounds in the venom transverse the blood-brain barrier to induce these central and long-lasting effects has been the subject of debate. In this article, we demonstrate that the wasp stings directly into the target ganglia in the head of its prey.

To prove this assertion, we produced “hot” wasps by injecting them with 14C radiolabeled amino acids and used a combination of liquid scintillation and light microscopy autoradiography to trace radiolabeled venom in the prey. To our knowledge, this is the first direct evidence documenting targeted delivery of venom by a predator into the brain of its prey.(Haspel *et.al.*, 2003)

CHAPTER THREE

Description of poisonous insects

3.0. Description of poisonous insects : (Shrivastava, 1993)(Sathe *et.al.*,2014)

Outline of poisonous insects orders and families :

A. Hymenoptera

- Vespidae
- Apidae
- Formicidae
- Ampulicidae

A. Hemiptera

- Cimicidae
- Reduvidae
- Pentatomidae
- Belastomatidae

C. Lepidoptera

- Syntomidae
- Erebidae
- Limacodidae
- Limantriidae
- Saturnidae
- Magalopygidae

D. Coleoptera

- Meloidae
- Staphylinidae

E. Blattodea

- Blattidae

F. Diptera

- Culicidae

- Tabanidae
- Simuliidae
- Oestridae
- Glossinidae

G. Siphonaptera

- Pulicidae

H. Sarcoptiformes

- Sarcoptidae

I. Araneae

- Theridiidae
- Sicariidae
- Eutichuridae
- Ctenidae & Hexathelidae

List of Poisonous insects :

1. Oriental hornet
2. Asian or Japanese giant hornet
3. Black tailed hornet
4. Common hornet
5. Emerald cockroach wasp
6. Giant honey bee
7. Indian honey bee
8. Western honey bee
9. Bullet ant
10. Carpenter ant
11. Driver ant
12. Weaver ant
13. Wood ant
14. Fire ant
15. Blister beetle
16. Rove beetle
17. Kissing bug
18. Giant water bug
19. Bed bug
20. Sting bug
21. Handmaiden moth caterpillar
22. Red hairy caterpillar
23. Slug caterpillar
24. Tussock moth caterpillar
25. Puss caterpillar
26. Nettle caterpillar

27. Circula silkmoth caterpillar
28. American cockroach
29. Oriental cockroach
30. Mosquitos
31. Horsefly
32. Blackfly
33. Botfly
34. Tsetseflly
35. Fleas
36. Lice
37. Itch mite
38. False widow spider
39. Brown recluse spider
40. Yellow sac spider
41. The red back spider
42. The Brazilian wardering spider
43. The black widow spider
44. The brown widow spider
45. The Sydney funnel-web spider
46. Six-eyed sand spider
47. Giant silkworm caterpillar
48. Io moth caterpillar

Description of poisonous insects :

3.1.Oriental hornet

Scientific name : *Vespa orientalis*

Family : Vespidae

Order : Hymenoptera

Features : Larger, deep brown with yellow band across abdomen, with petiolate abdomen

Life cycle : Several generations completed in a single year

Poison source : Sting and sting gland

Nature of poison : Serotonin, can kill man, cause swelling.

Description : The Oriental hornet, *Vespa orientalis*, is a social insect of the Vespidae family. It can be found in Southwest Asia, Northeast Africa, the island of Madagascar, Israel and parts of Southern Europe.Oriental hornets have also been found in a few isolated locations such as Mexico due to human introduction. The Oriental hornet lives in seasonal colonies consisting of caste system dominated by a queen.The hornet builds its nests underground and communicates using sound vibrations.The hornet has a yellow stripe on its cuticle (exoskeleton) which can absorb sunlight to generate a small electrical potential, and it has been suggested that this might help supply energy for digging. The adult hornet eats nectar and fruits and scavenges for insects and animal proteins to feed to their young. Because they are scavengers, the hornets may also serve as a transmitter of disease following consumption of infected plants. The hornets are a primary pest to honey bees, attacking bee colonies to obtain honey and animal proteins. The sting of an Oriental hornet can be quite painful to humans and some humans are allergic to stings.(Dvorak, 2006)

The adult hornet has two pairs of wings and a body measuring between 25 and 35 mm long. Males and workers are smaller in size than the queen. *Vespa orientalis* is a reddish-brown color and has distinctive thick yellow bands on the abdomen and yellow patches on the head between the eyes. They have very strong jaws and will bite if provoked. Females (workers and queen) have an ovipositor which is a specialized organ shaped like a tube that is used for laying eggs. The ovipositor extends from the end of the abdomen and is also used as a stinger. Drones (males) can be distinguished from workers (females) by the number of segments on their antenna. Drones have 13 segments while workers only have 12. The Oriental hornet looks similar to the European hornet (*Vespa crabro*) and should not be confused with the Asian giant hornet (*Vespa mandarinia*) of Eastern Asia.(Archer, 1998)

Stings :

Vespa stings are very painful to humans. They have smooth stingers that can be used multiple times. Humans can die from many stings suffered at once. Some people also suffer severe allergic reactions to stings

Symptom : A case of multiple hornet stings is described with a rapidly fatal course due to the combination of massive haemolysis, coagulopathy, rhabdomyolysis, hyperkalaemia, acute renal failure, encephalopathy, hepatotoxicity and hyperglycaemia. These features of systemic envenomation can all be attributed to the toxic properties of Oriental hornet venom described in in vitro and in vivo experimental studies. Greater awareness of these features, aggressive treatment of hyperkalaemia and early institution of treatments such as peritoneal dialysis and plasma exchange may prevent fatalities in such cases.(Korman *et.al.*, 1990)

3.2. Japanese giant hornet

Scientific name : *Vespa mandarinia japonica*

Family : Vespidae

Order : Hymenoptera

Characteristic feature : A single hornet can kill 40 honey bees per minutes

Description : In Japanese it is known as the *ōsuzumebachi.* Workers forage to feed their siblings. Their diet consists of a wide range of insects, including crop pests, and for this reason the hornets are regarded as beneficial. The workers dismember the bodies of their prey to return only the most nutrient-rich body parts, such as flight muscles, to the nest. There, the workers chew the prey into a paste before feeding the larvae which in return produce a fluid consumed by the workers. This fluid is known as vespa amino acid mixture (VAAM) Synthetic VAAM is being produced artificially as a dietary supplement, with claims that it can increase athletic performance. In many Japanese mountain villages, the hornet is considered a delicacy when fried.

Venom

The Japanese giant hornet is large and can be very aggressive if provoked. Its venom, which is injected by the 6.25 mm-long stinger, attacks the nervous system and damages the tissue of its victims. Tests involving mice found that the venom falls short of being the most lethal of wasp venom, having an LD_{50} of 4.0 mg/kg. In comparison, the deadliest wasp venom (at least to lab mice) by weight belongs to *Vespa luctuosa* at 1.6 mg/kg. The potency of the sting is due, rather, to the relatively large amount of venom injected. Being stung is extremely painful and can require hospitalization. Asian giant hornet stings can cause anaphylactic shock in allergic people but can still be lethal to people who are not allergic, provided the dose is sufficient. In China, where the hornet can also be found, the conventional wisdom is that people stung more than 10 times need medical help, and emergency treatment if stung more than 30 times. The stings can also cause renal failure. Thirty to forty people die in Japan every year after having been stung by bees and wasps (including the Japanese hornet). (Branigan, 2013)

The insect responsible for the deaths is the Asian giant hornet, which has a 6 millimeter stinger that injects its victim with venom containing a neurotoxin that is "powerful enough to dissolve human tissue," (Ingersoll, 2013)

3.3. Black tailed Hornet

Scientific name : *Vespa ducalis*

Family : Vespidae

Order : Hymenoptera

Features : Large, rust red and hairy with transparent wings with conical nest

Life cycle : Several generations completed in a year

Poison source : Sting and sting gland

Nature of poison : Serotonin, can kill man, cause swelling

Symptom : It creat yelp (pain). venom is pumped into the skin via a stinger at the back end of the insects. (Haddad, 2014) (Robert, 2017)

Description : This species specializes in attacking the nests of Polistines (paper wasps) and capturing the larvae to feed their own larvae. It is said to be almost exclusive in choice of prey, and very rarely takes other prey. It is said that a colony of *Vespa ducalis* needs at least 120 to 150 colonies of Polistine wasps to survive *Vespa ducalis*, like its near relative *Vespa tropica*, usually hunts singly among trees and shrubs in search of such wasp nests. When it locates one, it will land on the nest, immediately proceeding to pull out larvae and pupae, often tearing the cells in the process. The original occupants usually hide in a corner or flee the nest, never fighting back, like *Vespa tropica*, and unlike *Vespa soror*, this species seldom kills the original occupants, being content to drive them to one side so it can capture the larvae without resistance.

3.4. Common Hornet

Scientific name : *Polistes hebraeus* (Fab.)

Family : Vespidae

Order : Hymenoptera

Features : Medium sized, uniformly yellow with petiolate abdomen and with rounded nest

Life cycle : Several generations completed in single year

Poison source : Sting and sting gland

Nature of poison : Serotonin, can kill man, cause swelling

Symptoms : Painful and itchy for a few days. A sting is different to a bite because a venom is pumped into the skin via a stinger at the back end of the insect. Wasp are present mainly in the summer and can be most bothersome in late summer/autumn. (Haddad, 2014) (Robert, 2017)

Description : Wasps of the cosmopolitan genus *Polistes* (the only genus in the tribe Polistini) are the most familiar of the polistine wasps, and are the most common type of paper wasp in North America. It is also the single largest genus within the family Vespidae, with over 300 recognized species and subspecies. Their innate preferences for nest-building sites leads them to commonly build nests on human habitation, where they can be very unwelcome; although generally not aggressive, they can be provoked into defending their nests. All species are predatory, and they may consume large numbers of caterpillars, in which respect they are generally considered beneficial. The European paper wasp, *Polistes dominula*, was introduced into the US about 1981 and has quickly spread throughout most of the country, in most cases replacing native species within a few years. This species is very commonly mistaken for a yellow jacket, as it is black, strongly marked with yellow, and quite different from the native North American species of *Polistes*. The cuckoo wasp, *Polistes sulcifer*, is an obligate social parasite, whose only host is *P. dominula*. *Polistes annularis*, whose species name is Latin for "ringed", is also known for its distinctive red body color. *Polistes metricus* adults malaxate their insect prey by chewing them into a pulp, sucking out and ingesting the body fluids, then feeding the rest of the morsel to their larvae. The most widely distributed South American wasp species, *Polistes versicolor*, is particularly common in the southeastern Brazilian states. This social wasp is commonly referred to as the yellow paper wasp due to the distinct yellow bands found on its thorax and abdomen. *Polistes* wasps can be identified by their characteristic flight; their long legs dangle below their bodies, which are also more slender than a yellow jacket.(Carpenter , 2008)

3.5. Emerald cockroach wasp

Scientific name : *Ampulex compressa*

Family : Ampulicidae

Order : Hymenoptera

Features : Bluish metallic shining, about one inch long with ovipositor

Life cycle : Life cycle completed on cockroach body.

Poison source : Ovipositor / Sting

Nature of poison : Unidentified toxin cause itching, swelling.

Description : The emerald cockroach wasp or jewel wasp (*Ampulex compressa*) is a solitary wasp of the familyAmpulicidae. It is known for its unusual reproductive behavior, which involves stinging a cockroach and using it as a host for its larvae. It thus belongs to the entomophagous parasites(Banks, 2011)

3.6. Giant honey bee

Scientific name : *Apis dorsata*

Family : Apidae

Order : Hymenoptera

Features : Largest bee, 1.5 cm long hives 6 ft long, yield 36 kg honey/comb.

Life cycle : Life cycle completed within 15-20 days

Poison source : Sting & poison glands Acid & alkali glands

Nature of poison : Melittin Can kill man, Cause irritation and swelling, Enzymes Lecithinase & hyaluronidase

Description : *Apis dorsata*, the giant honey bee, is a honey bee of South and Southeast Asia, found mainly in forested areas such as the Terai of Nepal and even in Malaysia, Singapore and India. They are typically around 17–20 mm (0.7–0.8 in) long. Nests are mainly built in exposed places far off the ground, like on tree limbs, under cliff overhangs, and sometimes on buildings. These social bees are known for their aggressive defense strategies and vicious behavior when disturbed. Indigenous peoples have traditionally used this species as a source of honey and bees wax, a practice known as honey hunting. *Apis dorsata* is found from the Indian subcontinent to Southeast Asia. The greatest populations of *Apis dorsata* are found in China, Indonesia, India, Pakistan, and Sri Lanka. In the Philippines, which used to have one of the greatest populations of *Apis dorsata*, the populations have now become relatively rare due to deforestation and people's "mindsets" towards the bees. They mostly reside in tall trees in dense forests, but also build nests on urban buildings. These bees are tropical and in most places, they migrate seasonally. Individual colonies migrate between nesting sites during the transition from the rainy to dry seasons and occupy each nesting site for about 3–4 months at a time. Some recent evidence indicates these bees return to the same nest site, though most, if not all, of the original workers might be replaced in the process because workers usually live for less than two months. Furthermore, these bees build small combs that serve as temporary nests during their long migrations.(Maria et.al., 2005)

In Bornean rainforests, *Apis koschevnikovi* and *Apis dorsata* are the only honeybees that appear frequently at flowering canopy trees or baits. Even though they share most of the same rain forest habitat, they are still able to coexist. Their difference in size and tongue length help separate their resource use. (Starr, 1987)

3.7. Indian honey bee

Scientific name : *Apis indica*

Family : Apidae

Order : Hymenoptera

Features : Medium sized, 1 cm long, Make parallel comb, Yield 1.5 to 4.5 kg honey / comb

Life cycle : Life cycle completed in about 18 days

Poison source : Sting & sting gland

Nature of poison : Melittin & enzymes Cause swelling & irritations

Description : *Apis cerana indica*, the Indian honey bee, is a subspecies of Asiatic honey bee. It is one of the predominant bees found and domesticated in India, Pakistan, Nepal, Burma, Bangladesh, Sri Lanka, Thailand and mainland Asia. Relatively non-aggressive and rarely exhibiting swarming behavior, it is ideal for beekeeping. It is similar to the European honey bee (*Apis mellifera*), which tends to be slightly larger and can be readily distinguished. They usually build multiple combed nest in tree hollows and man-made structures. These bees can adapt to living in purpose-made hives and cavities. Their nesting habit means that they can potentially colonize temperate or mountain areas with prolonged winters or cold temperatures.It is one of the important pollinators for coconut palms; the other species are *Apis florea*, *Apis dorsata* and *Apis mellifera*,the European bee.(Thampan, 1981)

3.8. Western honey bee

Scientific name : *Apis mellifera*

Family : Apidae

Order : Hymenoptera

Features : Small sized. Make about 500 colonies, honey yield 45-181 kg

Life cycle : Several generations completed in a single year. Life cycle completed in 16 days

Poison source : Sting & sting gland

Nature of poison : Melittin

Description : The western honey bee or European honey bee (*Apis mellifera*) is the most common of the 7–12 species of honey bee worldwide. The genus name *Apis* is Latin for "bee", and *mellifera* means "honey-bearing", referring to the species' tendency to produce a large quantity of honey for storage over the winter. Like all honey bees, the western honey bee is eusocial, creating colonies with a single fertile female (or "queen"), many sterile females or "workers," and small proportion of fertile males or "drones." Individual colonies can house tens of thousands of bees. Colony activities are organized by complex communication between individuals, through both pheromones and the dance language. The western honey bee was one of the first domesticated insects, and it is the primary species maintained by beekeepers to this day for both its honey production and pollination activities. With human assistance, the western honey bee now occupies every continent except Antarctica. Because of its wide cultivation, this species is the single most important pollinator for agriculture globally. A number of pests and diseases threaten the honey bee, especially colony collapse disorder. Western honey bees are an important model organism in scientific studies, particularly in the fields of social evolution, learning, and memory; they are also used in studies of pesticide toxicity, to assess non-target impacts of commercial pesticides.(Kemp, 2014)

3.9. Bullet ant

Scientific name : *Paraponera clavata*

Family : Formicidae

Order : Hymenoptera

Symptom : Bullet ant is the largest of all ants in the world. They mostly found in rainforests of Nicaragua and Paraguay. Bullet ants named after their painful sting. After the bite victim would feel like being shot. In fact, the sting by a bullet ant is 30 times more painful than of a wasp or a honey bee. The one-inch sized bullet ant also called as '24-hour ant' by locals. It is because one full day pain followed by its sting. (Haddad, 2014) (Robert, 2017)

Description : Worker ants are 18–30 mm (0.7–1.2 in) long and resemble stout, reddish-black, wingless wasps. *Paraponera* is predatory, and like all primitive poneromorphs, does not display polymorphism in the worker caste; the queen ant is not much larger than the workers.

Sting :

The pain caused by this insect's sting is reported to be greater than that of any other hymenopteran, and is ranked as the most painful according to the Schmidt sting pain index, given a "4+" rating, above the tarantula hawk wasp, and according to some victims, equal to being shot, hence the name of the insect. It is described as causing "waves of burning, throbbing, all-consuming pain that continues unabated for up to 24 hours". Poneratoxin, a paralyzing neurotoxicpeptide isolated from the venom, affects voltage-dependent sodium ion channels and blocks the synaptic transmission in the central nervous system. It is being investigated for possible medical applications .(Gerritsen, 2001)

3.10. Carpender ants

Scientific name : *Camponotus compresus*

Family : Formicidae

Order : Hymenoptera

Features : Black, large, wingless, polymorphic mandibles with more than 5 teeth, unarmed

Life cycle : Queen can survive for several years (3-15 years)

Poison source : Mandible poison glands

Nature of poison : Formic acid, create wounds when bite cause irritations Symptom : Redness and swelling. Moderate pain. Allergic reactions are sneezing, wheezing, hives, nausea, vomiting, diarrhea, sudden anxiety, dizziness, difficulty breathing, chest tightness, itching or swelling of the face. (Haddad, 2014) (Robert, 2017)

Description : *Camponotus compressus* is a species of ant found in India and Southeast Asia. It is a frequent visitor to toilets as it consumes urea. It is one of the many species which tends plant-sap-sucking insects like aphids and tree hoppers. These ants stroke their antenna on the hind parts of these insects stimulating them to excrete a sugar rich liquid, called honeydew, which the ants consume. In return, they are known to protect the insects from predators like ladybugs. (Shetty, 1982)

3.11. Driver ant

Scientific name : *Dorylus gribodoi*

Family : Formicidae

Order : Hymenoptera

Description : *Dorylus*, also known as driver ants, safari ants, or siafu, is a large genus of army ants found primarily in central and east Africa, although the range also extends to southern Africa and tropical Asia. The term siafu is a loanword from Swahili, and is one of numerous similar words from regional Bantu languages used by indigenous peoples to describe various species of these ants. Unlike the New World members of the former subfamily Ecitoninae (now Dorylinae), members of this genus do form temporary anthills lasting from a few days up to three months. Each colony can contain over 20 million individuals. As with their New World counterparts, there is a soldier class among the workers, which is larger, with a very large head and pincer-like mandibles. They are capable of stinging, but very rarely do so, relying instead on their powerful shearing jaws.(Bolton, 2014)

3.12. Weaver ant

Scientific name : *Oecophylla smaragdina*

Family : Formicidae

Order : Hymenoptera

Features : Palp formula 5, 4; Mandible with 10 or more teeth; petiole reduced

Life cycle : Many generations completed in a single year

Poison source : Sting apparatus

Nature of poison : Iridomyrmecin

Description : Weaver ants or green ants (genus*Oecophylla*) are eusocialinsects of the family Formicidae (order Hymenoptera). Weaver ants are obligately arboreal and are known for their unique nest building behaviour where workers construct nests by weaving together leaves using larval silk. Colonies can be extremely large consisting of more than a hundred nests spanning numerous trees and contain more than half a million workers. Like many other ant species, weaver ants prey on small insects and supplement their diet with carbohydrate-rich honeydew excreted by small insects (Hemiptera). *Oecophylla* workers exhibit a clear bimodal size distribution, with almost no overlap between the size of the minor and major workers. The major workers are approximately 8–10 mm (0.31–0.39 in) in length and the minors approximately half the length of the majors. There is a division of labour associated with the size difference between workers. Major workers forage, defend, maintain, and expand the colony whereas minor workers tend to stay within the nests where they care for the brood and 'milk' scale insects in or close to the nests. *Oecophylla* weaver ants vary in color from reddish to yellowish brown dependent on the species. *Oecophylla smaragdina* found in Australia often have bright green gasters. These ants are highly territorial and workers aggressively defend their territories against intruders. Because of their aggressive behaviour, weaver ants are sometime used by indigenous farmers, particularly in southeast Asia, as natural biocontrol agents against agricultural pests. Although *Oecophylla* weaver ants lack a functional sting they can inflict painful bites and often spray formic acid directly at the bite wound resulting in intense discomfort. (Bolton, 2015)

3.13. Wood ants, mound ants, thatching ants, and field ants

Scientific name : *Formica* sp

Family : Formicidae

Order : Hymenoptera

Features : Apical margin of mandible with 8 teeth. 3 rd tooth of mandible is smaller than fourth

Life cycle : Many generations completed in a single year

Poison source : Sting apparatus

Nature of poison : Formic acid

Symptom : A small pink red mark on the skin. Red ant will attack when threatened. They have a fairly weak toxic in their sting. (Haddad, 2014) (Robert, 2017)

Description : *Formica* is a genus of ants of the familyFormicidae, commonly known as wood ants, mound ants, thatching ants, and field ants. *Formica* is the type genus of the Formicidae, and of the subfamily Formicinae. The type species of genus *Formica* is the European red wood ant *Formica rufa*. Ants of this genus tend to be between 4 and 8 mm long.(Klotz, 2008)

3.14. Fire ant

Scientific name : *Solenopsis* sp.

Family :Formicidae

Order : Hymenoptera

Symptom : There are 285 different species of fire ants in the world. Once disturbed, they would sting the intruder repeatedly. The fire ant sting is very painful also. A white pustule caused by fire ant sting last for weeks. Their venom also would cause several skin problems. Fire ants usually attack in the group that contains ten to hundreds of ants. The venom of fire ants also result in allergic reaction. (Haddad, 2014) (Robert, 2017)

3.15. Blister beetle

Scientific name : *Mylabria pustulata or Hycleus sp.*

Family : Meloidae

Order : Coleoptera

Features : Blackish with yellow or red zigzag bands on elytra, elongated

Life cycle : Hypermetamorp hosis, one generation in a single year

Poison source : Accessory glands, blood

Nature of poison : Acidic substance cantharidin

Symptom : Blisters or welt (it caused by a chemical called cantharidin). Symptom occurs within a few hours of contact and no lasting skin damage. (Haddad, 2014) (Robert, 2017).

Description : *Hycleus* is a genus of blister beetle belonging to the Meloidae family found in Africa and Asia. They have been confused with the genus name *Mylabris*. Adults feed mainly on flowers from a wide range of plant families. The first larval instar is an active triungulin form that is a predator of soft insects such as aphids. While the young are often beneficial to crops by suppressing other plant feeders, the adults can be a problem when present in large numbers. Flower feeding leads to lower yield and this can be a problem in some leguminous crops. They are however easily controlled by manual collection. (Bologna, 2014)

3.16. Rove beetles

Scientific name : *Paederus sp.*

Family : Staphylinidae

Order : coleoptera

Symptom : The hemolymph of the *Paederus* beetles contains multiple toxins, with the most important being pederin, a crystalline amide with potent vesicant and caustic actions that is soluble in water and alcohol. The toxins of the *Paederus* spp. cause intense erythema, edema, and vesicles, which converge to form blisters. The burning and itching symptoms of envenomation by the *Paederus* are more intense than those caused by *Lytta* and *Epicauta* beetles(Haddad *et.al.*, 2014)

Description : *Paederus* is a genus of small beetles of the familyStaphylinidae ("rove beetles"). With 622 valid species assigned by 1987 to the subtribe Paederina (*Paederus* and its close allies), and with all but 148 within *Paederus* itself, the genus is large. Due to toxins in the hemolymph of some species within this genus, it has given its name to paederus dermatitis, a characteristic skin irritation that occurs if one of the insects is crushed against skin. That name, Paederus dermatitis, is a poor choice because, decades earlier, the affliction had been called dermatitis linearis, a name that works in all languages, not just English, because of its Latin origin; the name Paederus dermatitis is also inappropriate because it has shown to be caused by (a) only a few species of the genus Paederus, but (b) also a few species that belong to closely related genera (that are not *Paederus*) within the subtribe Paederina. A scholarly paper in 2002 suggested that a *Paederus* species could have been responsible for some of the ten Plagues of Egypt described in the Bible's Book of Exodus. Like other beetles (Coleoptera), rove beetles have hardened forewings that cover the flight wings. At one time, the rove beetle group was known as "Brachyptera" (short wings), because their flight wings are folded under short elytra. *Paederus* species are widely distributed around the world. They are much more brightly colored than other rove beetles, with metallic blue- or green-colored elytra and many with bright orange or red on the pronotum and the basal segments of the abdomen. These bright colors may be an example of aposematism, a warning signal to potential predators. Although most adult rove beetles avoid daylight, *Paederus* species are active during the day and attracted to bright lights after nightfall. *Paederus* eggs are laid singly, in moist habitats. Larvae go through two instars before pupation. Both larvae and adults are predatory on other insects. Because of their preference for moist soil, large numbers of *Paederus* beetles may be attracted to irrigated farmland, where they provide some benefit by eating herbivorous insects but can cause problems for people working in fields or grassy areas (Mullen *et.al.*, 2011)

Paederus are nocturnal and attracted by incandescent and fluorescent lights and as a result, inadvertently come into contact with human.(Frank, 1987).

Hemolymph of the beetle contain paederin(latigaza) which is released on crushing of the insect onto the skin due to the reflex of brushing away the insects. Paederin is an amid with two tetrahydropyran rings and makes up approximately 0.025 % of an insect's weight.(Davalos, 1999)

3.17. Kissing bug

Scientific name: *Tritoma* sp

Family : Reduvidae

Order : Hemiptera

Features : Head longer, subcylindrical or convex above, antennae inserted at or near the middle of anteocular portion

Life cycle : Life cycle completed in one year

Poison source : Salivary gland

Nature of poison : Toxin aenesthetic, anticoagulin.

Description : The members of Triatominae ,a subfamily of Reduviidae, are also known as conenose bugs, kissing bugs, assassin bugs, or vampire bugs. Other local names for them used in the Latin Americas include barbeiros, vinchucas, pitos and chinches. Most of the 130 or more species of this subfamily are haematophagous, i.e. feeds on vertebrate blood; a very few species feed on other invertebrates (Sandoval *et.al.* 2000).

They are mainly found and widespread in the Americas, with a few species present in Asia, Africa, and Australia. These bugs usually share shelter with nesting vertebrates, from which they suck blood. In areas where Chagas disease occurs (from the southern United States to northern Argentina), all triatomine species are potential vectors of the Chagas disease parasite *Trypanosoma cruzi*, but only those species (such as *Triatoma infestans* and *Rhodnius prolixus*) that are well adapted to living with humans are considered important vectors. Proteins released from their bites have been known to induce anaphylaxis in sensitive and sensitized individuals.(Klotz, 2010)

3.18. Giant water bug

Scientific name : *Lethocerus americanus*

Family : Belastomatidae

Order : Hemiptera

Description : Insects of the family Belostomatidae cause painful stings in humans (Picado, 1936). The water cockroaches, arauembóias, or giant water bugs are worlwide insects classified into two main genera (*Lethocerus* and *Belostoma*). These large insects are found in freshwater habitats and they are voracious predators, capable of hunting tadpoles and fish(Haddad *et.al.*, 2012). Giant water bugs can reach 10cm in size. They have a short stout beak that is used to pierce their prey and inject toxic saliva composed of enzymes that can liquefy the tissues of the prey(Cardoso, 2009). There are reports of lysophospholipids in the saliva of the species *Belostoma anurum* that can cause paralysis in the neuromuscular junctions of the prey. These insects can produce very painful lesions in humans and may also carry infections. The treatment for the sting is symptomatic. (Haddad *et.al.*, 2010) (A.S.Menke, 1960).

Belostomatidae is a family of freshwater hemipteraninsects known as giant water bugs or colloquially as toe-biters, Indian toe-biters, electric-light bugs, alligator ticks, or alligator fleas (in Florida). They are the largest insects in the order Hemiptera, and occur worldwide, with most of the species in North America, South America, Northern Australia, and East Asia. They are typically encountered in freshwater streams and ponds. Most species are at least 0.75 in (2 cm) long, although smaller species also exist. The largest are members of the genus *Lethocerus*, which can exceed 4.75 in (12 cm) and nearly reach the length of some of the larger beetles in the world. Giant water bugs are a popular food in parts of southeast Asia.(Goodwyn, 2006)

The multiple ways venom is used by heteropterans suggests that further study will reveal heteropteran venom components with a wide range of bioactivities that may be recruited for use as bioinsecticides, human therapeutics, and pharmacological tools.(Walker, 2016)

3.19. Bed bug

Scientific name : *Cimex lectularius*

Family : Cimicidae

Order : Hemiptera

Features : Flat bodied, mahogany brown, suck blood of man.

Life cycle : Life cycle completed in 20-30 days. 4 generations produced in a single year

Poison source : Glands

Nature of poison : Itching, inflammatory wale (T.V. Sathe *et.al.*,2015)

Symptom : Red welt, swelling, red rash. Initial burning sensation and bed bud bites are often very itchy and sometimes appear in a straight line. It is the world's greatest hitchikers and they breed very quickly. (Haddad, 2014) (Robert, 2017)

Description : Bed bugs are parasiticinsects of the cimicid family that feed exclusively on blood. *Cimex lectularius*, the common bed bug, is the best known as it prefers to feed on human blood; other *Cimex* species specialize in other animals, e.g., bat bugs, such as *Cimex pipistrelli* (Europe), *Cimex pilosellus* (Western United States), and *Cimex adjunctus* (entire Eastern United States).The name bed bug derives from the preferred habitat of *Cimex lectularius*: warm houses and especially near or inside beds and bedding or other sleep areas. Bed bugs are mainly active at night, but are not exclusively nocturnal. They usually feed on their hosts without being noticed. A number of adverse health effects may result from bed bug bites, including skin rashes, psychological effects, and allergic symptoms. Bed bugs are not known to transmit any pathogens as disease vectors. Certain signs and symptoms suggest the presence of bed bugs; finding the adult insects confirms the diagnosis. Bed bugs have been known as human parasites for thousands of years. At a point in the early 1940s, they were mostly eradicated in the developed world, but have increased in prevalence since 1995, likely due to pesticide resistance, governmental bans on effective pesticides, and international travel. Because infestation of human habitats has begun to increase, bed bug bites and related conditions have been on the rise as well.(Kolb, 2009)

3.20. Sting bug

Scientific name : *Halyomorpha halys*

Family : Pentatomidae

Order : Hemiptera

Description : The adults are approximately 1.7 centimetres (0.67 in) long and about as wide, forming the shield shape characteristic of other stink bugs. They are various shades of brown on both the top and undersides, with gray, off-white, black, copper, and bluish markings. Markings unique to this species include alternating light bands on the antennae and alternating dark bands on the thin outer edge of the abdomen. The legs are brown with faint white mottling or banding. The stink glands are located on the underside of the thorax, between the first and second pair of legs, and on the dorsal surface of the abdomen.(Jacobs, 2011)

The insects of the family Pentatomidae (stink bugs, marias-fedidas, fedes-fedes) cause contact skin injuries that are similar to those associated with *Paederus* beetles. The crushing of these hemipterans against the skin causes vesicular and erythematous plaques on exposed areas, which are accompanied by a burning sensation and pruritus. Treatment is similar to that employed in the linear dermatitis caused by vesicant beetles.(Haddad *et.al.*, 2002)

3.21 Handmaiden moth

Scientific name : *Ceryx godarti*

Family : Syntomidae

Order : Lepidoptera

Features : Larva light brown, hairy; moth with 6 and 3 clear transparent spots on fore and hind wings respectively.

Life cycle : Life cycle completed within 47-48 days

Poison source : Hairs

Nature of poison: Formic acid (Sathe *et.al.*, 2014)

Description : The handmaiden moth, is a moth of family Arctiidae, subfamily Ctenuchinae. The systematics of the subfamily is under revision. It was described by Pieter Cramer in 1780. It is well distributed in Sikkim, Khasi hills and throughout India, Sri Lanka, Myanmar, and Hong Kong. The moth has a wingspan of 34 mm. The frons and collar are yellow with the metathorax having a yellow streak. The first abdominal segment has a yellow band which is sometimes obsolescent. The forewing has large hyaline patches, one filling the cell, another filling nearly the whole interno-median interspace, one at junction of veins 2 and 3, two subapical, and two submarginal. In the form *S. i. sargania*, there is a long streak between veins 5 and 6. In others it is reduced to a spot or may be lacking entirely. The hindwing has a postbasal hyaline patch extending hardly (or not at all) beyond the cell. The tips of the antennae and proximal joints of the tarsi are white. The spots of the forewing vary considerably in size. The male individual is slender and long abdomen than female.(Hampson, 1892)

3.22. Red hairy caterpillar

Scientific name : *Amsacta albistriga*

Family : Erebidae

Order : Lepidoptera

Features : Larva hairy

Life cycle : Life cycle completed in 30 days.

Poison source : Hairs

Nature of poison : Formic acid

Description : The red hairy caterpillar, is a moth of the family Erebidae. It is found in southern India. The wingspan is 40–50 mm (1.6–2.0 in). The larvae defoliate various agricultural crops. After about thirty to forty days of feeding the larvae burrow into the soil to pupate.

3.23. Slug caterpillars

Scientific name : *Natada velutina*

Family : Limacodidae

Order : Lepidoptera

Features : Larva beautiful coloured with green, blue and pink spots and with 8 branched spines, 4 anteriorly and 4 posteriarly. Moth is red, brown with wing expanse of 3 inch.(Epstein, 1993)

Life cycle : Life cycle completed on mango.

Poison source : Spines

Nature of poison : Formic acid extremely irritant (Hampson, 1892)(Murphy, 2010)

3.24. Tussock moths

Scientific name : *Euproctis* Sp

Family : Limantriidae

Order : Lepidoptera

Features : Larva blackish brown, hairy.

Life cycle : Life cycle completed in about 30 days.

Poison source : Hairs

Nature of poison : Formic acid irritant.

Description : Palpi obliquely porrect (projecting forward), reaching beyond the frons. Antennae bipectinated (comb like on both sides) in both sexes, where branches are long in males each with a spine to keep it in position with regard to the contiguous branch. Mid tibia with one pair of long spurs and hind tibia with two pairs. Female has a large anal tuft. Forewings with veins 3, 4 and 5 from near angle of cell. Vein 6 from or from below upper angle. Veins 7 to 10 are stalked, where vein 10 being given off towards apex. Hindwings with vein 3 and 4 stalked or from angle of cell. Vein 5 from above angle, and veins 6 and 7 stalked.(Hampson, 1892)

3.25. Puss caterpillar

Scientific name : *Megalopyge opercularis*

Family : Megalopygidae

Order : Lepidoptera

Description :

The southern flannel moth, *Megalopyge opercularis* (J. E. Smith) (Insecta: Lepidoptera: Zygaenoidea: Megalopygidae), is an attractive small moth that is best-known because of its larva, the puss caterpillar, which is one of the most venomous caterpillars in the United States (Bishopp 1923, Mallakh.E.I *et.al.*, 1986, Hossler 2010, Khalaf 1975). Larvae: The number of instars is uncertain and may be variable. Bishopp (1923) stated that there are probably five or six instars. and gave the following approximate lengths for the first four and last instars: 1st instar: 1.5 mm, 2nd instar: 2.3 mm, 3rd instar: 3.1 mm, 4th instar: 3.6mm, mature larva: 2.54 cm (1 inch).

Davidson (1967) reported similar dimensions. It seems that there may have been a misidentification of later instars by these authors based on the huge size difference reported between the fourth and final instars. Khalaf (1975) reported that there are 8 to 10 instars.

The integument of first and second instars is yellow but becomes pale greenish white to white in later instars. Larvae become progressively more "hairy" with each molt. All instars have rows of verrucae raised sclerites with radiating setae (Gordh *et.al*, 2001) that bear hollow spines each of which has a venom gland at its base (Foot 1922). The spines are obscured by the long soft setae in the late instars. Late instars have a hairy tail. The color of late instars is somewhat variable. (Bishopp, 1923) Occasionally, in outbreak years, puss caterpillars are sufficiently numerous to defoliate some trees (Bishopp 1923). However, their main importance is medical. In Texas, they have been so numerous in some years that schools in San Antonio in 1923 and Galveston in 1951 were closed temporarily because of stings to children (Diaz, 2005).

The venomous spines of puss caterpillars are hollow and each is equipped with a venom gland at its base (Foot 1922). All larval instars, as well as exuviae, may sting but the toxicity of the stings increases with increasing size of the larvae (Davidson, 1967).

Foot (1922) reported that some individuals react more severely to stings than others, and the severity of the sting varies with the thickness of the skin where the sting occurs The sting produces an immediate intense burning pain followed the appearance of a red grid-like pattern on the skin that matches the pattern of the venomous spines on the caterpillar. Swelling and sometimes also lymphadenopathyfollow. In addition to the characteristic localized symptoms, more general systemic manifestations may also occur including headache, fever, nausea, vomiting, tachycardia, low blood pressure, seizures and more rarely, abdominal pain, muscle spasms and convulsions.

The venom is not well-characterized but it has been shown to possess hemolytic activity, and there is evidence that it is proteinaceous based primarily on its precipitation by 75% saturated ammonium sulfate and the fact that it is inactivated by digestion with proteolytic enzymes (trypsin, pepsin, or chymotrypsin has reviewed common treatments for puss caterpillar stings. Remedies that may be helpful in some cases include removing broken spine tips from the skin with tape, applying ice packs, use of oral antihistamine, application of hydrocortisone cream to the site of the sting, systemic corticosteroids, and intravenous calcium gluconate. (Picarelli *et.al.*, 1971) (Eagleman, 2008)

3.26. Nettle caterpillar

Scientific name : *Parasa lipida*

Family : Limantriidae

Order : Lepidoptera

Features : Larva segmented above and bears spinous tubercles.

Life cycle : Life cycle completed on castor and mango leaves.

Poison source : Spines

Nature of poison : Formic acid produces dermatitis

Description : *Parasa lepida*, the nettle caterpillar or blue-striped nettle grub, is a moth of the Limacodidae family that was described by Pieter Cramer in 1799. It is a native minor pest found in the Indo-Malayan region, including

India, Sri Lanka, Vietnam, Malaysia and Indonesia. It is an introduced pest to urban trees in western Japan. In the male, the head is greenish, with red brown at the sides. The thorax is green with a brown stripe on the vertex. Abdomen brown. Forewings are pale green, resembling the colour of a pea plant. There is a red-brown basal patch on the costa. Outer area is reddish brown, widest at inner margin. Hindwing yellowish at base, reddish brown towards margin. Legs have pale tipped joints. In the female, the reddish-brown stripe on the thorax is much wider and nearly the whole of the hindwing is reddish brown. Larva pale green, whitish or bright yellowish green on the dorsal surface. There are three green bands throughout the body. Sub-dorsal and sub-lateral series of short spinous tubercles, the spines of the anterior and posterior tubercles tipped with red. Cocoon purple brown. Eggs are flat and overlap each other. Eggs are covered by a transparent cement.(Hampson, 1892)(Smith,2016)

3.27. Cricula silkmoth

Scientific name : *Cricula trifenestrata*

Family : Saturnidae

Order : Lepidoptera

Features : Larva clothed with spines.

Life cycle : Life cycle completed on leaves of mango.

Poison source : Spines

Nature of poison : Unidentified toxin body decay as in leprosy.

Description : The wingspan is 65–100 mm. Adults are on wing from May to June with a possible second brood from August to September. Male is brown, ochreous, yellowish to reddish. Forewings are consisted with a waved anti-medial dark line and a small hyaline spot beyond the end of the cell, with one or two others above it. The upper one is a dark spot. Hindwings with oblique line continued to the inner margin before the middle. There is a hyaline spot beyond the cell. Ventral side is much purple. Female is red. There are three large irregularly shaped hyaline spots beyond the cell of the forewing, often with one or two small sides inside them. Larva is blackish brown in color. There are six setiferous tubercles in each somite from 2nd to 11th. First somite and anal claspers are crimson colored. Legs and prolegs are brown colored. Cocoon composed of bright golden yellow silk firmly united into a network. The larvae have been recorded on *Anacardium*, *Mangifera*, *Spondias*, *Careya*, *Bischofia*, *Canarium*, *Quercus*, *Cinnamomum*, *Machilus*, *Persea*, *Acrocarpus*, *Ziziphus*, *Malus*, *Prunus*, *Pyrus*, *Salix* and *Schleichera* species. (Hampson, 1892)

3.28. American cockroach

Scientific name : *Periplanta americana*

Family : Blattidae

Order : Dictyoptera

Features : Flat bodied, brownish, with filiform antenna and cerci.

Life cycle : One generation completed in a single year.

Poison source : Glands.

Nature of poison : Allergic substance, cause linear dermatitis, edema of eye, urticaria.

Description : The American cockroach (*Periplaneta americana*), also colloquially known as the waterbug, but not a true waterbug since it is not aquatic, or misidentified as the palmetto bug (see Florida woods cockroach for the differences), is the largest species of common cockroach, and often considered a pest. It is also known as the ship cockroach, kakerlac, and Bombay canary. Despite the name, none of the *Periplaneta* species is endemic to the Americas; *P. americana* was introduced to the United States from Africa as early as 1625. They are now common in tropical climates because human activity has extended the insect's range of habitation, and are virtually cosmopolitan in distribution as a result of global commerce. American cockroaches are also known as plagues in the warm Mediterranean coast of Spain, as well as in southern Spain and southern Portugal (starting from Barcelona to the Algarve) and in the Canary Islands; where the winters are mild/warm and frost-free, and the summers are hot. (Jacobs, 2012)

Risk to humans:

The odorous secretions produced by American cockroaches can alter the flavor of food. Also, if populations of cockroaches are high, a strong concentration of this odorous secretion can be present. Cockroaches can pick up disease-causing bacteria, such as Salmonella, on their legs and later deposit them on foods and cause food infections or poisoning. House dust containing cockroach feces and body parts can trigger allergic reactions and asthma in certain individuals.(Jacobs, 2012)

3.29. Oriental cockroach

Scientific name : *Blattella orientalis*

Family : Blattidae

Order : Dictyoptera

Features : Flat bodied, brownish, shorter than *P. americana*.

Life cycle : Life cycle completed in 6 weeks.

Poison source : Glands

Nature of poison : Allergic substance, cause linear dermatitis, edema of eye, urticaria.

Description The oriental cockroach (*Blatta orientalis*), also known as the waterbug, is a large species of cockroach, adult males being 18–29 mm (0.71–1.14 in) and adult females being 20–27 mm (0.79–1.06 in). It is dark brown or black in color and has a glossy body. The female has a somewhat different appearance from the male, appearing to be wingless at casual glance, but is brachypterous, having non-functional wings just below her head. She has a wider body than the male. The male has long wings, which cover two-thirds of the abdomen and are brown in color, and has a narrower body. Both sexes are flightless. The female oriental cockroach looks somewhat similar to the Florida woods cockroach, and may be mistaken for it. Originally endemic to the Crimean Peninsula and the region around the Black Sea and Caspian Sea, its distribution is now cosmopolitan.(Robinson et.al., 2005)

3.30. Mosquito

Scientific name : Culex sp.

Family : Culicidae

Order : Diptera

Nature of poison : Anesthetic and anticoagulin Symptom : hard bumps,it can be puffy with a red dot in the middle,stings may appear as small as blisters instead of bumps. Mosquito bites usually present themselves as red, raised lumps that can be incredibly itchy. Mosquitos are incredibly good at biting and stealing your blood without you even knowing. They produce an anesthetic when they bite. Mosquitoes are usually active from the spring through to the autumn but can hide over the winter.(Logan, 2017)

Description : *Culex* is a genus of mosquitoes, several species of which serve as vectors of one or more important diseases of birds, humans and other animals. The diseases they vector include arbovirus infections such as West Nile virus, Japanese encephalitis, or St. Louis encephalitis, but also filariasis, and avian malaria. They occur worldwide except for the extreme northern parts of the temperate zone, and are the most common form of mosquito encountered in some major US cities such as Los Angeles. Depending on the species, the adult *Culex* mosquito may measure from 4–10 mm (0.2–0.4 in). The adult morphology is typical of flies in the suborder Nematocera with the head, thorax, and abdomen clearly defined and the two fore wings held horizontally over the abdomen when at rest. As in all Diptera capable of flight, the second pair of wings are reduced and modified into tiny, inconspicuous halteres. Formal identification is important in mosquito control, but it is demanding and requires careful measurements of bodily proportions and noting the presence of absence of various bristles or other bodily features. In the field informal identification is more often important, and the first question as a rule is whether the mosquito is anopheline or culicine. Given a specimen in good condition, one of the first things to notice is the length of the maxillary palps. Especially in the female, palps as long as the proboscis are characteristic of anopheline mosquitoes. Culicine females have short palps. Anopheline mosquitoes tend to have dappled or spotted wings, while Culicine wings tend to be clear. Anopheline mosquitoes tend to sit with their heads low and their rear ends raised high, especially when feeding, while Culicine females keep their bodies horizontal. Anopheline larvae tend to float horizontal at the surface of the water when not in motion, whereas culicine larvae float with head low and only the siphon at the tail held at the surface.(Syed, 2009)

3.31. Horsefly

Scientific name : *Tabanus sulcifrons*

Family : Tabanidae

Order : DipteraSymptom : Bleeding and reddish bumps. they have razor sharp jaws and cause a very painful bite, soreness and itchiness. It can take longer to recover from a horsefly bite as they break the skin when they bite, so make sure you keep the bite clean. Horseflies are found throughout the summer months especially around stables and farmyards on hot sunny days. (Logan, 2017) (Haddad, 2014)

Description : The larvae are predaceous and grow in semiaquatic habitats. Female horse-flies can transferblood-borne diseases from one animal to another through their feeding habit. In areas where diseases occur, they have been known to carry equine infectious anaemia virus, some trypanosomes, the filarial worm*Loa loa*, anthrax among cattle and sheep, and tularemia. As well as making life outdoors uncomfortable for humans, they can reduce growth rates in cattle and lower the milk output of cows if suitable shelters are not provided. The outlines of the adult insect's head and wings are visible through the pupa, which has seven moveable abdominal segments, all except the front one of which bears a band of setae. The posterior end of the pupa bears a group of spine-like tubercles. Horse-flies *Haematopota pluvialis* feeding on a horse's head .Some species, such as deer flies and the Australian March flies, are known for being extremely noisy during flight, though clegs, for example, fly quietly and bite with little warning. Tabanids are agile fliers; *Hybomitra* species have been observed to perform aerial manoeuvres similar to those performed by fighter jets, such as the Immelmann turn.(Squitier, 2015)(Axtell, 1975)(Chainey, 1993)

Horse-fly bites :

Humans find horse-fly bites painful. Usually, a weal (raised area of skin) occurs around the site, and other symptoms may include urticaria (a rash), dizziness, weakness, wheezing, and angioedema (a temporary itchy, pink or red swelling occurring around the eyes or lips); a few people experience an allergic reaction. The site of the bite should be washed and a cold compress applied. Scratching the wound should be avoided and an antihistamine preparation can be applied. In most cases, the symptoms subside within a few hours, but if the wound becomes infected, medical advice should be sought.(Squitier, 2015)

3.31. Blandford fly or blackfly

Scientific name : *Simulium posticatum*

Family : Simuliidae

Order : Diptera

Symptom : It is a 2-3 mm blood sucking blackfly. These insects tend to fly at less than half a meter from the ground. So most people are bitten on the legs. (Haddad, 2014) (Robert, 2017)

Description : The Blandford fly (*Simulium posticatum*) is a species of black fly, a biting insect found in Europe, Turkey and western Siberia. It spends its larval stage in the weedbeds of slow flowing rivers and when the fly emerges, the female seeks a blood meal before mating. It usually bites the lower legs causing pain, itching and swelling. Scratching the irritated areas can lead to breaks in the skin, after which secondary infection may set in.The Blandford fly's English common name derives from a major outbreak of people being bitten around the town of Blandford Forum in Dorset, England, in the 1960s and 1970s. In a four-week period during the spring of 1972, some 600 people were estimated to have visited their doctors in Blandford to be treated for insect bites. In the late 1980s, Dorset County Council asked the Institute for Freshwater Ecology, then based in Wareham, Dorset, to investigate a means of ameliorating the problem. They suggested using a biological insecticide, *Bacillus thuringiensis israelensis* (Bti), which was sprayed into the weed beds, resulting in the destruction of 80–90% of the Blandford fly larvae and a corresponding reduction in the numbers of people bitten. Indeed, it is reported that the number of people bitten has dropped to less than one hundredth of those affected in 1989. Recently, the fly has begun affecting people in other parts of southern England, including built up areas, probably encouraged by water features. Singer Mollie King and golfer Ian Poulter have both been affected by bites, with the latter having to pull out of the French Open.(Laurance, 2010)

3.33. Bot Fly

Scientific name : *Dermatobia hominis*

Family : Oestridae

Order : Diptera

Symptom : The larve bore into muscle tissue of the mamamls. It causes myiasis. The larvae of botflies are internal parasites of mammals. Unfortunately, the dangerous larvae also live beneath human's skin and cause horrible effects. The human bot flies mostly found across Central and South America. 'Myiasis' known parasite infestation makes severe changes in skin tissues. The young female bot flies laid eggs within the skin of mammals. The larvae penetrate through skin and lives in subdermal zones of human skin for more than 60 days. The patients could feel the movement of larvae beneath their skin. Once larvae development gets complete, it leaves out of the body. (Haddad, 2014) (Robert, 2017)

3.34. Tsetse Flies

Scientific name : *Morsitans sp.*

Family : Glossinidae

Order : Diptera

Symptom : TseTse flies is a deadliest biting insect native to Africa. They mainly feed on the blood of vertebrates. The extreme dangerous insects inject potent toxin on each string. It is estimated that about half a million people lost their life by the attack of tsetse flies in Africa. At the primary stage, the venom of tsetse flies would make sleeping sickness on the victim. But it may lead to fatality without proper treatment. (Haddad, 2014) (Robert, 2017)

Description : Tsetse are biological vectors of trypanosomes, meaning that in the process of feeding, they acquire and then transmit small, single-celled trypanosomes from infectedvertebratehosts to uninfected animals. Some tsetse-transmitted trypanosome species cause trypanosomiasis, an infectious disease. In humans, tsetse transmitted trypanosomiasis is called sleeping sickness. In animals, tsetse-vectored trypanosomiases include *nagana*, *souma*, and *surra* according to the animal infected and the trypanosome species involved. The usage is not strict and while *nagana* generally refers to the disease in cattle and horses it is commonly used for any of animal trypanosomiasis. Trypanosomes are animal parasites, specifically protozoans of the genus *Trypanosoma*. These organisms are about the size of red blood cells. Different species of trypanosomes infect different hosts. They range widely in their effects on the vertebrate hosts. Some species, such as *T. theileri*, do not seem to cause any health problems except perhaps in animals that are already sick. Some strains are much more virulent. Infected flies have an altered salivary composition which lowers feeding efficiency and consequently increases the feeding time, promoting trypanosome transmission to the vertebrate host.[These trypanosomes are highly evolved and have developed a lifecycle that requires periods in both the vertebrate and tsetse hosts.(Abbeele, 2010)

3.35. Fleas

Scientific name : *Xenopsylla sp.*

Family : Pulicidae

Order : Siphonaptera

Symptom : Red spot surrounded by reddened haloes and often found on legs and feet and very itchy. Fleas are external parasites that suck blood from humans, birds, reptiles and wild and domestic animals. The fleas could cause itching spots on the skin of hosts. Fleas only have a size of the tip of a pen and reproduce very quickly. Every female flea lay 2000 eggs within their life span. There are 2000 known species of flies in the world. Young fleas can consume the volume of blood that over 15 times their body weight. The flea bites on human body result in red bumps. They commonly found around waist, knees, and elbows. The bite of fleas are very itchy, and it may also lead to infection. (Haddad, 2014) (Robert, 2017)

Description : Fleas are small flightless insects that form the order Siphonaptera. As external parasites of mammals and birds, they live by consuming the blood of their hosts. Adults are up to about 3 mm (0.12 in) long and usually brown. Bodies flattened sideways enable them to move through their host's fur or feathers; strong claws prevent them from being dislodged. They lack wings, and have mouthparts adapted for piercing skin and sucking blood and hind legs adapted for jumping. The latter enable them to leap a distance of some 50 times their body length, a feat second only to jumps made by froghoppers. Larvae are worm-like with no limbs; they have chewing mouthparts and feed on organic debris. Over 2,500 species of fleas have been described worldwide. The Siphonaptera are most closely related to the snow scorpionflies (Boreidae), placing them within the endopterygote insect order Mecoptera. Fleas arose in the early Cretaceous, most likely as ectoparasites of mammals, before moving on to other groups including birds. Each species of flea is more or less a specialist on its host animal species: many species never breed on any other host, though some are less selective. Some families of fleas are exclusive to a single host group: for example, the Malacopsyllidae are found only on armadillos, the Ischnopsyllidae only on bats, and the Chimaeropsyllidae only on elephant shrews. The oriental rat flea, *Xenopsylla cheopis*, is a vector of *Yersinia pestis*, the bacterium which causes bubonic plague. The disease was spread by rodents such as the black rat, which were bitten by fleas that then infected humans. Major outbreaks included the Plague of Justinian and the Black Death, both of which killed a sizeable fraction of the world's population. (Gullan, 2016)

3.36. Lice

Scientific name : *Fahrenholzia pinnata*

Family : Polyplacidae

Order : Phthiraptera

Symptom : Bites in public hair, armpit or eyebrow. Bluish-grey skin reactions sores and small red bumps. Itching that often gets worse at night. Tiny white eggs called nits may be found in hair. (Haddad, 2014) (Robert, 2017)

Description : Louse (plural: lice) is the common name for members of the order Phthiraptera, which contains nearly 5,000 species of wingless insect. Lice are obligate parasites, living externally on warm-blooded hosts which include every species of bird and mammal, except for monotremes, pangolins, bats and cetaceans. Lice are vectors of diseases such as typhus. Chewing lice live among the hairs or feathers of their host and feed on skin and debris, while sucking lice pierce the host's skin and feed on blood and other secretions. They usually spend their whole life on a single host, cementing their eggs, which are known as nits, to hairs or feathers. The eggs hatch into nymphs, which moult three times before becoming fully grown, a process that takes about four weeks. Humans host three species of louse, the head louse, the body louse and the pubic louse. The body louse has the smallest genome of any known insect; it has been used as a model organism and has been the subject of much research.(Parry, 2013)

3.37. Itch mite / scabies

Scientific name : *Sarcoptes scabiei*

Family : Sarcoptidae

Order : Sarcoptiformes

Symptom : Pimple-like rashes usually on wrist, elbow, armpit, nipple, waist, belt-line, buttocks and between the fingers. Small raised lines on surface of the skin. Intence itching that worsens in the evening. Numbness, tingling and swelling around the sting site. (Haddad, 2014) (Robert, 2017)

Description : Scabies, previously known as the seven-year itch, is a contagious skin infestation by the mite*Sarcoptes scabiei*. The most common symptoms are severe itchiness and a pimple-like rash. Occasionally, tiny burrows may be seen in the skin. In a first ever infection a person will usually develop symptoms in between two and six weeks. During a second infection symptoms may begin in as little as 24 hours. These symptoms can be present across most of the body or just certain areas such as the wrists, between fingers, or along the waistline. The head may be affected, but this is typically only in young children. The itch is often worse at night, Scratching may cause skin breakdown and an additional bacterial infection of the skin. Scabies is caused by infection with the female mite*Sarcoptes scabiei var. hominis*. The mites burrow into the skin to live and deposit eggs. The symptoms of scabies are due to an allergic reaction to the mites. Often, only between 10 and 15 mites are involved in an infection. Scabies is most often spread during a relatively long period of direct skin contact with an infected person (at least 10 minutes) such as that which may occur during sex. Spread of disease may occur even if the person has not developed symptoms yet. Crowded living conditions, such as those found in child-care facilities, group homes, and prisons, increase the risk of spread. Areas with a lack of access to water also have higher rates of disease. Crusted scabies is a more severe form of the disease. It typically only occurs in those with a poor immune system and people may have millions of mites, making them much more contagious. In these cases, spread of infection may occur during brief contact or by contaminated objects. The mite is very small and usually not directly visible. Diagnosis is based on the signs and symptoms. A number of medications are available to treat those infected, including permethrin, crotamiton, and lindane creams and ivermectin pills. Sexual contacts within the last month and people who live in the same house should also be treated at the same time. Bedding and clothing used in the last three days should be washed in hot water and dried in a hot dryer. As the mite does not live for more than three days away from human skin, more washing is not needed. Symptoms may continue for two to four weeks following treatment. If after this time symptoms continue, retreatment may be needed. Scabies is one of the three most common skin disorders in children, along with ringworm and bacterial skin infections. As of 2015, it affects about 204 million people (2.8% of the world population). It is equally common in both sexes. The young and the old are more commonly affected. It also occurs more commonly in the developing world and tropical climates. The word scabies is from *Latin:* scabere, "to scratch".Other animals do not spread human scabies. Infection in other animals is typically caused by slightly different but related mites and is known as sarcoptic mange.(Ferri et.al., 2010)

3.38. False widow spider

Scientific name : *Steatoda nobilis*

Family : Theridiidae

Order : Araneae

Symptom : Two puncture marks close together. The widow spiders are showing muscle cramps and pain, increased blood pressure, sweating, skin rash. The violin spiders are showing anemia, blood in the urine, fever, rash, nausea, vomiting and even coma(rare)(Orkin, 2017) (Haddad, 2014) (Robert, 2017)

3.39. Brown recluse spider

Scientific name : *Loxosceles reclusa*

Family : Sicariidae

Order : Araneae

Symptom : Reddening and swelling, blister may appear at the bite site. Mild skin irritation(itching), fever, convulsions,nausea and muscle pain. A small number of bites produce severe lesions as seen in the above picture. The physical bite depends on the amount of venom injected and an individuals sensitivity to it. (Haddad, 2014) (Robert, 2017)

Brown Recluse Spider is a violin shaped marking on the top of their cephalothorax, which is a fused head and thorax. This is why Brown Recluse Spiders are sometimes called saddleback or violin spiders. But what really sets them apart is that they only have six eyes instead of eight like most spiders. Brown Recluse Spiders are only found in central and southeastern United States and they are fairly small, about the size of a penny. However, for being a small spider they can pack a powerful bite. Luckily, 90 percent of bites don't require medical attention and usually don't scar. For the other 10 percent who are sensitive to the spider's venom, well, it defnitely isn't a fun experience. First, a white blister will grow around the bite and the tissue may become hard. The area of the bite can develop bluegray or blue-white patches that have ragged edges and are surrounded by redness. Even more frightening is that a bite can develop into a volcano lesion. This happens when the tissue around the bite becomes gangrenous and this results in a nasty open wound. As for how big these wounds get, they can be as big as a human hand. Usually, it takes eight weeks to heal, which is a long time to recover from anything, but it sounds like a lifetime to have a gaping, gangrenous wound on your body. Luckily, fatal Brown Recluse Spider bites are incredibly rare. There were only two recorded deaths between 2004 and 2014.

3.40. Yellow Sac Spiders

Scientific name : *Cheiracanthium sp.*

Family : Eutichuridae

Order : Araneae

Symptom : Yellow Sac Spiders are part of the Cheiracanthium genus, and there are different species found throughout the world, like the United States, Australia, Europe, and Japan. Both males and females are about half an inch big and are often pale in color. One interesting thing to note about Yellow Sac Spiders is that they love the smell of gasoline. This problem actually led Mazda to recall 52,000 cars in March 2011 because Yellow Sac Spiders were building webs in the emissions system. Besides just being annoying to car manufacturers, Yellow Sac Spiders are also venomous. The immediate bite of the spider is incredibly painful and can lead to redness and swelling. Luckily, unless someone has an allergy to the venom, there are rarely any lasting effects. (Haddad, 2014) (Robert, 2017)

Description : *Cheiracanthium* are usually pale in colour, and have an abdomen that can range from yellow to beige. Both sexes range in size from 5 to 10 mm. Some yellow sac spiders are attracted to the smell of volatiles in gasoline. Of all "common house spiders", they are the only species whose tarsi do not point either outward (like *Tegenaria*) or inward (like *Araneus*), and are therefore easy to identify.

Venom :

Cheiracanthium venom is purportedly necrotic, and it could cause a small lesion in humans. However, both the necrotic nature and severity of the spider's bite have been disputed. Because of the possibly necrotic nature of the wound, MRSA infection is a danger and victims are advised to seek medical treatment. Painful bites may be incurred from species such as *C. punctorium* in Europe, *C. mildei* in Europe and North America, *C. inclusum* in the Americas, *C. lawrencei* in South Africa and *C. japonicum* in Japan. (Platnick, 2007)

3.41. The Redback Spider

Scientific name : *Latrodectus hasseltii*

Family : Theriididae

Order : Araneae

Symptom : The Redback Spider is a close relative to Black Widow Spiders, but the Redback is only found in Australia and they are recognizable because they have a red stripe on their back. The red is much darker on females than on the males. They are a medium sized spider, and their bodies are about the size of a large pea. Luckily, most Redback Spider bites aren't serious. Only about 250 bites every year need antivenom. A person usually experiences sweating (especially near the bite), nausea, muscle weakness and vomiting. We're pretty sure that these symptoms would have been extremely uncomfortable for the man whose penis was bitten by a Redback spider in April 2016 while he was using a public toilet. Luckily, he was released from the hospital after a few hours of sheer panic and terror. Since the introduction of the antivenom in 1956, there has been one possible death caused by a Redback spider bite, which would make it the first death from any spider in Australia since 1979. In April 2016, 22-year-old Jayden Burleigh was bitten by a Redback spider under his left arm. He was hospitalized for four days and given antibiotics. He died three days after being released from the hospital, so it's unclear if his death was caused by the bite or some other factor. (Haddad, 2014) (Robert, 2017)

Venom:

The redback and its relatives in the genus *Latrodectus* are considered dangerous, alongside funnel-web spiders (*Atrax* and *Hadronyche*), mouse spiders (*Missulena*), banana spiders (*Phoneutria*) and recluse spiders (*Loxosceles*). Venom is produced by holocrine glands in the spider's chelicerae (mouth parts). Venom accumulates in the lumen of the glands and passes through paired ducts into the spider's two hollow fangs. The venom of the redback spider is thought to be similar to that of the other *Latrodectus* spiders. It contains a complex mixture of cellular constituents, enzymes and a number of high-molecular-weight toxins, including insect toxins and a vertebrate neurotoxin called alpha-latrotoxin, which causes intense pain in humans. In vertebrates, alpha-latrotoxin produces its effect through destabilisation of cell membranes and degranulation of nerve terminals, resulting in excessive release of neurotransmitters, namely acetylcholine, norepinephrine and GABA. Excess neurotransmitter activity leads to clinical manifestations of envenomation, although the precise mechanisms are not well understood. Acetylcholine release accounts for neuromuscular manifestations, and norepinephrine release accounts for the cardiovascular manifestations. Female redbacks have an average of around 0.08–0.10 mg of venom, and experiments indicate that the median lethal dose (LD_{50}) for mice at room temperature is 10–20% of this quantity (0.27–0.91 mg/kg based on the mass of the mice used), but that it is considerably more deadly for mice kept at lower or higher temperatures. Pure alpha-latrotoxin has an LD_{50} in mice of 20–40 µg/kg. The specific variant of the vertebrate toxin found in the redback was cloned and sequenced in 2012, and was found to be a sequence of 1180 amino acids, with a strong similarity to the equivalent molecule across the *Latrodectus mactans* clade. The syndromes caused by bites from any spiders of the *Latrodectus* genus have similarities; there is some evidence there is a higher incidence of sweating, and local and radiating pain with the redback, while black widow envenomation results in more back and abdominal pain, and abdominal rigidity is a feature common with bites from the west coast button spider (*Latrodectus indistinctus*) of South Africa. One crustacean-specific and two insect-specific neurotoxins have been recovered from the Mediterranean black widow (*L. tredecimguttatus*), as have small peptides that inhibit angiotensin-1-converting enzyme; the venom of the redback, although little-studied, likely has similar agents.(Rubin et.al., 2012)(Wiener,1956)

3.42. Brazilian Wandering Spider

Scientific name : *Phoneutria sp.*

Family : Ctenidae

Order : Araneae

Symptom : There are eight different types of Brazilian Wandering Spiders, and as you may have guessed, they are predominantly found in Brazil, with a few species spread out across Latin America. They are about two inches long with a leg span of about six inches. Brazilian Wandering Spiders differ from other spiders because they don't lure prey into a web. Instead, they spend most of their day in cool areas. Then at night, they hunt on the floors of the forests. They either wait to ambush their prey or directly attack them; making them some of the most aggressive spiders in the world. However, they are not aggressive towards humans. Actually, none of the spiders on the list are. Most of the time spiders bite humans because they feel trapped and/or cornered. That being said, you definitely do not want to frighten a Brazilian Wandering Spider. After a bite, the person may experience a burning sensation in the area of the bite, along with goosebumps and sweats. About 30 minutes later, the person's blood pressure may increase or decrease and their heartbeat may go faster or slow down. Nausea, abdominal cramping, blurred vision, hypothermia, vertigo, and excessive sweating are also symptoms of a bite from a Brazilian Wandering Spider. Another unusual side effect is that in males, is that it can cause a painful erection that could last several hours. Needless to say, when a Brazilian Wandering Spider was found in a bag of bananas purchased by a family in Leicester, England, the tabloids had a field day writing horror stories about the terrifying venomous spider that causes erections. The good news is that in most cases, the Brazilian Wandering Spider doesn't secrete enough venom in a bite to cause serious damage. A study from 2008 found that from all bites, only 2.6 percent needed antivenom. However, it is still important to seek medical attention after a bite because 10 recorded deaths have been contributed to the spider. (Haddad, 2014) (Robert, 2017)

The genus *Phoneutria* includes some of the relatively few species of spiders known to present a threat to humans. Danger to humans is not merely a question of toxicity, but requires the capacity to deliver the venom, a sufficient quantity of venom, a disposition that makes a bite likely and proximity to human habitation. The actual incidence of death or serious injury must also be considered. Spider mouthparts are adapted to envenom very small prey; they are not well-adapted to attacking large mammals such as humans. Some experts believe that various spiders like *Phoneutria* can deliver a "dry" bite to purposely conserve their venom, as opposed to a more primitive spider like *Atrax* that usually delivers a full load. A study in March 2009 suggests that *Phoneutria* inject venom in approximately one-third of their bites, and only a small quantity in one-third of those cases. Another study similarly suggested that only 2.3 percent of bites (mainly in children) were serious enough to require antivenom. Other studies, as cited in the Wolfgang Bücherl studies, showed that the toxicity of *Phoneutria* venom was clearly more potent than both *Latrodectus* and *Atrax*. Research in this area is hindered by the difficulty of identifying particular species. Nevertheless, there are well-attested instances of death. In one case, a single spider killed two children in São Sebastião. The spider was positively identified as a *Phoneutria* by Wolfgang Bücherl. Despite their reputation, there are multiple studies that call into question their capacity for fatal human envenomation, though some of these are labeled with a level of uncertainty, as *Phoneutria* are often confused with other genera of ctenids, lycosids or other large labidognatha spiders. Of the eight described species, *P. nigriventer* and *P. fera* most frequently receive mention in mass-media publications. *P. nigriventer* is the species responsible for most cases of venom intoxication in Brazil because it is commonly found in highly populated areas of southeastern Brazil, such as the states of São Paulo, Minas Gerais, Rio de Janeiro and Espírito Santo. The species *P. fera* is native to the northern portion of South America in the Amazon of Brazil, Venezuela, Ecuador, Peru and the Guyanas.These spiders' wandering nature is another reason they are considered so dangerous. In densely populated areas, *Phoneutria* species usually search for cover and dark places to hide during daytime, leading it to hide in houses, clothes, cars, boots, boxes and log piles, where they may bite if accidentally disturbed.(Herzig et.al., 2002)

3.43. The Black Widow Spider

Scientific name : *Latrodectus sp.*

Family : Theridiidae

Order : Araneae

Symptom : One of the most notorious spiders is the Black Widow Spider. They are found in regions that are temperate, dark, and dry throughout much of the world, including the United States, South America, Africa, southern Europe and Asia, and Australia. The females are the most distinctive of the species for several reasons. The first is that they are about twice the size of males, and they are about 1.5 inches long. They have an hourglass shaped body that is shiny. Also, on the underside on the right abdomen, there is a distinctive red hourglass marking. They get their unique name because after mating, the female eats the male. Most of the time people who are bitten by Black Widow Spiders don't suffer any serious symptoms. However, according to National Geographic, their venom is 15 times stronger than a rattlesnake, so if they bite and inject a lot of venom, then the person could be in a lot of trouble. At first, the person will feel a sharp pain at the area of the bite, like a pinprick. The bite area will redden and swell. Then, as early as 15 minutes after the bite, pain will spread throughout the body, especially in the chest and abdomen. The muscles in those areas will start to cramp because of severe spasms. This may lead to dificulty breathing because the diaphragm can become paralyzed. Black Widow Spiders are rarely deadly to healthy adults, there is less than a one percent chance of a bite being fatal, but they can be dangerous to children, the elderly, and sick people. (Haddad, 2014) (Robert, 2017)

Latrodectus is a genus of spiders in the family Theridiidae, most of which are commonly known as widow spiders. The genus contains 31 recognized species distributed worldwide, including the North American black widows (*L. mactans*, *L. hesperus*, and *L. variolus*), the button spiders of Africa, and the Australian redback spider. Species vary widely in size. In most cases, the females are dark-coloured and readily identifiable by reddish markings on the abdomen, which are often (but not always) hourglass-shaped. The venomous bite of these spiders is considered particularly dangerous because of the neurotoxin latrotoxin, which causes the condition latrodectism, both named after the genus. The female black widow has unusually large venom glands and its bite can be particularly harmful to humans. However, despite the genus' notoriety, *Latrodectus* bites are rarely fatal. Only female bites are dangerous to humans.(Breene et.al., 1985)

Due to the presence of latrotoxin in their venom, black widow bites are potentially dangerous and may result in systemic effects (latrodectism) including severe muscle pain, abdominal cramps, hyperhidrosis, tachycardia, and muscle spasms. Symptoms usually last for 3–7 days, but may persist for several weeks. Each year, about 2,200 people report being bitten by a black widow, but most recover within 24 hours with medical treatment (male spiders produce the toxins to help with their own hunting, but they make such a diluted version that they are not harmful to most people). Also, many people who are bitten develop few symptoms since the spider may not inject its venom. Black widows are not especially aggressive spiders, and they rarely bite humans unless startled or otherwise threatened. Contrary to popular belief, most people who are bitten suffer no serious damage, l*et.al*one death. Fatal bites were reported in the early-20th century mostly with *Latrodectus tredecimguttatus*, the Mediterranean black widow. Since the venom is not likely to be life-threatening, antivenom has been used as pain relief and not to save lives. However, a study demonstrated that standardized pain medication, when combined with either antivenom or a placebo, had similar improvements in pain and resolution of symptoms.(Isbister et.al., 2014)

3.44. The Brown Widow Spider

Scientific name . *Latrodectus geometricus*

Family : Theridiidae

Order : Araneae

Symptom : As you've probably already guessed by its name, the Brown Widow Spider is a close relative of the Black Widow Spider. The Brown Widow Spider is different in color, ranging from gray to dark brown, whereas Black Widows are brown to black. They also have an hourglass marking on their abdomen. They are about 1 inch to 1.5

inches long and are usually found in tropical areas. However, since 2003, their population has been exploding in Southern California. They hide in places that don't see much human traffic or undisturbed areas like piles of brush or wood. The venom of the Brown Widow Spider is actually more toxic than the Black Widow Spider. One man who was bitten in the neck said that the pain was so bad after 10 minutes that it felt like he was hit with a sledgehammer. The symptoms start with redness and swelling. This is followed by cramps and spasms that can last for several hours. Luckily, there are no recorded deaths from Brown Widow Spiders. (Haddad, 2014) (Robert, 2017)

Like all *Latrodectus* species, *L. geometricus* has a neurotoxic venom. The venom acts on nerve endings causing the very unpleasant symptoms of latrodectism. However, brown widow bites are usually not very dangerous; usually much less dangerous than those of *L. mactans*, the black widow. The effects of the toxin are usually confined to the bite area and surrounding tissue, unlike the black widow's. Mere toxicity of the venom is not the only factor in dangerousness. Brown widow bites are minor compared to black widow bites because they cannot deliver the same amount of venom as the black widow. The LD_{50} of *L. geometricus* venom has been measured in mice as 0.43 mg/kg, and separately again as 0.43 mg/kg (with a 95% confidence interval of 0.31-0.53).(Brown et.al., 2012)

3.45. The Sydney Funnel-Web Spider

Scientific name : *Atrax robustus*

Family : Hexathelidae

Order : Araneae

Symptom : There are 43 different kinds of Funnel-Web Spiders and they are all found in Australia. The funnel web spiders get their names because of the distinctive style in which they build their webs. They find wet ground and then build a horizontal web with a funnel in the center of it that often leads into the ground or some other type of shelter. The spider waits in the funnel until prey lands on it and then springs out, and drags the prey down. What sets the Funnel-Web Spider apart from other spiders that build horizontal webs is that it uses irregular strings of web to set up "tripwires" near the entrance of the web. This gives the spider an advanced warning that prey is nearby. One of the most dangerous of the Funnel-Web Spiders is the Sydney Funnel- Web Spider, specifically the males. They are generally found within a 62 mile radius of Sydney and are medium sized. Usually, the largest are 0.4 to 2 inches long. However, one at the Australian Reptile Park (which is used to milk venom for antivenom) is called Big Boy, and is a whopping four inches long. What makes Big Boy so terrifying is that the bigger the spider, the more venom they produce, and Sydney Funnel-Web Spider venom is some of the most dangerous in the world. In fact, if it were to bite you in your chest, it could kill you in 15 minutes. However, most of the time people are bitten on their limbs. The male's venom contains a polypeptide called Robustoxin which affects the nervous system of humans and primates, but doesn't really affect other mammals. What happens when you first get bit is that it will be extremely painful because the Sydney Funnel-Wed Spider has long fangs and the venom has a high pH level. After the bite, the person may start drooling because they have numbness around the mouth and excess saliva. They may also have a copious amount of tears. Soon they will have problems breathing and may lose consciousness. The good news is that there is an antivenom, which was developed in 1981, and no one has died since its discovery. Before that, it was responsible for 13 recorded deaths. The bite of a Sydney funnel-web is initially very painful, with clear fang marks separated by several millimetres. The size of fangs is responsible for the initial pain. In some cases the spider will remain attached until dislodged by shaking or flicking it off.(White, 2013) (Haddad, 2014) (Robert, 2017)

Venom:

Funnel-web spider venom contains a compound known as atracotoxin, an ion channel inhibitor, which makes the venom highly toxic for humans and other primates. However, it does not affect the nervous system of other mammals. These spiders typically deliver a full envenomation when they bite, often striking repeatedly, due to their defensiveness and large chitinouscheliceral fangs. There has been no reported case of severe envenoming by female funnel-web spiders, which is consistent with the finding that the venom of female specimens is less potent than the venom of their male counterparts. In the case of severe envenomation, the time to onset of symptoms is less than one hour, with a study about funnel-web spider bites finding a median time of 28 minutes. This same study revealed that children are at a particular risk of severe funnel-web envenoming, with 42% of all cases of severe envenoming being children. There is at least one recorded case of a small child dying within 15 minutes of a bite from a Sydney funnel-web spider.(Isbister et.al., 2005)

3.46. Six-eyed Sand Spider

Scientific name : *Sicarius hahni*

Family : Sicariidae

Order : Araneae

The Six-eyed Sand Spider is a relative of the Recluse Spider and it is only found in the deserts of southern Africa. They are medium size spiders, they are about 0.3 inches to about 0.6 inches long, and they are covered in little hairs called setae. These hairs pick up particles of sand and it makes a camouflage for them. In addition to covering themselves in sand, the Sixeyed Sand Spider also hides by *burying* itself in the sand. When its prey gets too close, the spider ambushes it. No one is exactly sure what happens when a Six-eyed Sand Spider bites someone. There are only two suspected cases of envenomation, but they couldn't be confirmed. However, studies in labs have shown that the venom is quite dangerous because of a toxin called cryotoxin. Once it enters the body, it starts to destroy tissue and organs. So it ends up acting like sulfuric acid and eats away at the flesh, creating a lesion. Shortly after being bitten, hemorrhaging will start and the toxin spreads to the kidneys and liver, leading to death. Currently, there is no antivenom. Fortunately, Six-eyed Sand Spiders are notoriously shy. Perhaps we should keep our distance from them, unless you want to become evidence of what damage a bite could do to humans. (Haddad, 2014) (Robert, 2017)

Venom

Toxicology studies have demonstrated that the venom is particularly potent, with a powerful hemolytic/necrotoxic effect, causing blood vessel leakage, thinning of the blood and tissue destruction. Sicarius bite treatment should be directed, as with all cytotoxic bites, at prevention of secondary infection and combating Disseminated intravascular coagulation (DIC) if it develops.No anti-venom exists for it.(Occupational Health Southern Africa, 2005)

3.47. Giant silkworm caterpillar

Scientific name : *Lonomia oblique*

Family : Saturniidae

Order : Lepidoptera

Venom: Disseminated intravascular coagulation occurs as the toxin interacts with the victim's body. One serious effect on envenomed victims is hemorrhage syndrome. First described by Arocha-Pinango and Layrisse in Venezuela in 1967, the hemorrhagic diathesis caused in humans by touching the *Lonomia* species begins with inflammatory changes at the site of envenoming, followed by systemic symptoms such as headache, fever, vomiting, and malaise. After 24 hours, a severe bleeding disorder ensues, leading to ecchymosis, hematuria, pulmonary, and intracranial hemorrhages, and acute renal failure.(Kowacs, et.al., 2006)

3.48. Io moth :

Scientific name : *Automeris io*

Family : Saturnidae

Order : Lepidoptera

Sting : Virtually the entire bodies of larvae are protected by venomous spines. The spines have been described in detail by Battisti et al. (2011) and Gilmer (1925). Some spines are tipped with points and others with setae (Gilmer 1925). When spines penetrate the skin, the tips break off and release the venom. Spine tips may remain in the skin causing further irritation (Hossler et al. 2008). Battisti et al. (2011) hypothesized that as embedded spine tips begin to break down in the skin, the chitin may invoke an inflammatory response. Chitin particles of about 10-40 µm in size are known to invoke pro-inflammatory immune responses, but smaller chitin particles may actually be anti-inflammatory (Alvarez 2014, Da Silva et al. 2009). The points on Io moth caterpillar spines that are likely to remain in the skin are roughly 12 µm in length - right at the threshold of the inflammatory size. However, their irritating effect may be merely mechanical or due to small amounts of venom remaining in the points.

CHAPTER FOUR

Identification and Diagnosis of Insect bites

4.0. Identification and Diagnosis of Insect bites :

- Yellow jackets‘ nests are made of a paper-maché material and are usually located underground, but can sometimes be found in the walls of frame buildings, cracks in masonry or woodpiles.
- Honeybees and bumble bees are non-aggressive and will only sting when provoked. However, Africanized honeybees "killer bees" found in the Southwestern U.S. are more aggressive and may sting in swarms. Domesticated honeybees live in man-made hives, while wild honeybees live in colonies or "honeycombs" in hollow trees or cavities of buildings.
- Paper wasps’ nests are usually made of a paper-like material that forms a circular comb of cells which opens downward. The nests are often located under eaves, behind shutters, or in shrubs or woodpiles.
- Hornets are usually larger than yellow jackets. Their nests are gray or brown, football-shaped and made of a paper material similar to that of yellow jackets‘ nests. Hornets’ nests are usually found high above ground on branches of trees, in shrubbery, on gables or in tree hollows.
- Fire ants build nests of dirt in the ground that may be quite tall (18 inches) in the right kinds of soil.

The diagnosis of a reaction to a bite or sting is usually obvious from the history. The doctor will perform a physical examination to look for effects of the bite or sting on various parts of the body. If you can safely provide an example of what bit or stung you, it can be very helpful to the medical caregiver to determine both diagnosis and treatment. Examination of the skin, respiratory system, cardiovascular system, and oral cavity are particularly important to determine both diagnosis and treatments. To identify the disease that is transmitted by biting or stinging bugs or insects, blood tests are usually required; once the definitive diagnosis is made (for example, Lyme disease, West Nile virus or malaria), specific treatments then can be started.(Davis, 2016)(Ellis, 2003)

Skin testing for honeybee, wasps, hornets, and yellow jackets :

Diagnostic testing should be performed when the history is consistent with the indications for VIT. Before ordering venom skin tests or venom-specific IgE level measurement, the clinician should discuss with the patient the likely recommendation depending on whether the test results are positive or negative and whether the potential benefit might exceed the potential harm (eg, anxiety, altered lifestyle, and decreased quality of life) from the results of diagnostic evaluation. Diagnostic testing is recommended based on the clinical history, even when the systemic reaction was many years or decades earlier, because the risk of reaction can persist for long periods of time. Even when there has been a sting without a reaction occurring after the systemic reaction, the risk of anaphylaxis can persist.(Franken, 1994)

In vitro tests can also be used for detection of venom-specific gE antibodies in those subjects who cannot undergo skin testing. This includes patients with dermatographism or severe skin disease. Skin tests are generally the preferred initial testing method. Up to 20% of subjects with positive venom skin test responses have undetectable serum levels of specific IgE antibodies (negative in vitro test result). However, recent studies have demonstrated that 10% to 20% of patients with negative skin test responses have positive in vitro test results when using assays capable of detecting low levels of venom-specific IgE antibodies. Indications for obtaining these studies are discussed in the preceding section on skin tests. The utility of laboratory methods is also dependent on the reliability of the methods used by clinical laboratories; the clinician is advised to become familiar with differences in results by using different assays and different laboratories.(Hamilton, 2001)

CHAPTER FIVE

First aid and Treatment

5.0. First aid and Treatment :

5.1.Emergency Kits for Insect Stings

Highly-sensitive persons should have two emergency kits prescribed for them by their physician within easy access at all times. One kit should be carried at all times and the other kept in the family car. It is best to store kits in a cool, dry place (refrigeration) with easy access. The kit contains one sterile syringe of Epinephrine (adrenalin) EPIPEN, ready for injection, four chewable, yellow tablets of Chlortrimeton (antihistamine), two sterile alcohol swabs for cleaning the injection site and one tourniquet. Inject the syringe into the thigh (subcutaneously) under the skin as soon as the first sting symptoms show. A tourniquet placed above the sting site, when on an arm or leg just tight enough to obstruct blood return but not so tight as to stop circulation, will help until medical treatment is obtained. Loosen the tourniquet every 10 minutes.(Ohio State University Extension Fact Sheet,1991)

i. Poisonous insects be carefully collected with the help of insect net and containers and killed in dipping into kerosinised water
ii. Caterpillars have been controlled by 0.15% Carbaryl spray and by using parasitoids & predators (Sathe, 2014).
iii. Bees and Wasps have been controlled by 0.5% dichlorvos or 1.5% Baygon spray.
iv. Ants have been controlled by 5% Diazinon and destroying their nests. (Sathe *et.al.*,2015)
v. For all insects bites and stings, keep them clean by washing with warm water and soap. Place a cold towel over the area to help reduce swelling. Antihistamines is good choice for insect stings and bites (Logan, 2017)

Mechanism of the allergic response to venom. a (left). An antibody response is triggered by the presence of venom in the body and these antibodies attach to the mast cells. b (right). When venom comes into contact with the antibodies, the mast cells respond by releasing substances such as histamine, which cause swelling and inflammation (Heddle *et.al*,,2014).

5.2.Treatment :

i) Sting apparatus be removed from body immediately.
ii) Apply juice of flowers of periwinkle and juice of leaves of marigold or tulsi to wounds.
iii) Anti allergic drugs like - Cetrizine be advised.
iv) Treat the wound with Ice and Sodium bicarbonate.
v) Against caterpillar venomous wound, baking soda, carbolated vaseline, ammonia or calamine lotion be treated.
vi) Against cockroach poisoning smooth lotion and antiallergic drugs be used.

5.3.Action plan for Anaphylaxis :

5.3.1.Signs Of Mild To Moderate Allergic Reaction :

- Swelling of lips, face, eyes
- Hives or welts
- Tingling mouth
- Abdominal pain, vomiting (ASCIA 2016)

5.3.2.Action For Mild To Moderate Allergic Reaction :

- For insect allergy - flick out sting if visible
- For tick allergy - freeze dry tick and allow to drop off
- Stay with person and call for help
- Locate EpiPen® or EpiPen® Jr adrenaline autoinjector
- Phone family/emergency contact(ASCIA 2016)

5.3.3.Signs Of Anaphylaxis (Severe Allergic Reaction) :

- Difficult/noisy breathing
- Swelling of tongue
- Swelling/tightness in throat
- Wheeze or persistent cough
- Difficulty talking and/or hoarse voice
- Persistent dizziness or collapse
- Pale and floppy (young children) (ASCIA 2016)

5.4.Action For Anaphylaxis :

a. Lay person flat - do NOT allow them to stand or walk

    - If unconscious, place in recovery position
    - If breathing is difficult allow them to sit

b. Give EpiPen® or EpiPen® Jr adrenaline autoinjector
c. Phone ambulance*- 000 (AU) or 111 (NZ)
d. Phone family/emergency contact
e. Further adrenaline doses may be given if no response after 5 minutes
f. Transfer* person to hospital for at least 4 hours of observation (ASCIA 2016)

If in doubt give adrenaline autoinjector Commence CPR at any time if person is unresponsive and not breathing normally (EpiPen® is prescribed for children over 20kg and adults. EpiPen Jr® is prescribed for children 10-20kg) always give adrenaline autoinjector first, and then asthma reliever puffer if someone with known asthma and allergy to food, insects or medication has sudden breathing difficulty (including wheeze, persistent cough or hoarse voice) even if there are no skin symptoms.

5.5.Treatment of Anaphylaxis

Treatment is directed at limiting the absorption of noxious material and by countering the adverse reactions. The ABCD's of resuscitation should be followed while simultaneously calling ambulance .

The ABCD's refer to:

- A – airway
- B – breathing
- C – circulation
- D – drug treatment

Drug Administration Record:

1. Epinephrine (Adrenalin) 1:1000 aqueous solution: Administer 0.01 mL/kg (maximum 0.5 mL per injection) intramuscularly (IM). Epinephrine, at the same dose as the initial one, can be repeated at 10-15 minute intervals to a maximum of 3 doses.

The following approximate dosages (0.01 mL/kg) Epinephrine (Adrenalin) administered:

may be used:

2 to 6 months

6 to 12 months

12 to 18 months

18 months to 4 years

1. years
2. to 9 years

10 to 13 years

≥14 years

0.07 mL

0.07-0.1 mL

0.1-0.15 mL

0.15 mL

0.20 mL 0.30 mL

0.40 mL

0.50 mL

1st dose Amount: ________________ mL (if given) Time: ________________

Site: ________________

2nd dose Amount: ________________ mL (if given) Time: ________________

Site: ________________

3rd dose Amount: ________________ mL (if given) Time: ________________ Site: ________________

2.

Diphenhydramine (Benadryl) (50 mg/mL). Administer intramuscularly (IM). A *maximum* dose of 50 mg (or 1.00 mL) at site other than inoculation. See pediatric dosages below. Do Not Repeat.

The following approximate dosages may be used:

Under age 2 years 0.25 mL Age 2 to 4 years 0.50 mL

Age 5 to 11 years 0.50 to 1.00 mL

≥12 years 1.00 mL

Diphenhydramine (Benadryl) administered:

Only One Dose Amount: ___________ Time: ________________________

Site: ________________________

The above Drug Administration Record is to be reproduced and included in each anaphylaxis kit.**5.7.Anaphylaxis Kit – Each kit should contain the following items:**

- 1 Page of "Drug Management Guidelines for Management of Suspected Anaphylactic Shock in Children and Adults" (taped to the inside of the box lid)
- 3 x 1 mL ampoules of epinephrine (1:1000 aqueous solution)
- 1 x 1 mL vials of diphenhydramine (50 mg/mL)
- 3 x 1 mL syringes with safety engineered needles* (various lenghts with 25G)
- pocket mask
- 5 alcohol swabs
- Sphygmomanometer (optional)

- Stethoscope (optional)

Up to date contact information for the Public Health Supervisor and Medical Officer(s) of Health. Length of needle to be selected appropriate to patient size and body mass. (Suggest: Needle gauge: 25G, needle lenghts: 3 x 1″; 3 x 5/8″; 3 x 1.5″) .The kits can be stored at room temperature and should be closed with an elastic to ensure the drugs are not exposed to light which can cause them to deteriorate. Additionally, the kits require regular verification to replace drugs before the expiry date.(Ohio State University Extension Fact Sheet,1991)

5.8.History of VIT:

Allergen immunotherapy for hay fever was discovered at St Mary's Hospital in London by Leonard Noon in 1911, and the first randomized controlled trial of this treatment for hay fever, also at St Mary's Hospital, proved its efficacy in 1954.49,50 The first report of VIT was described in 1925, where the whole crushed body of a wasp was used. Whole-body extract VIT continued to be used for many years, until it was shown to be ineffective in a randomized controlled trial. It was not until 1978 that an effective modality of VIT was developed. This used venom extracted from venom sacs, and was shown to be highly effective in a randomized controlled trial. Since that time, extracted venom has been used for immunotherapy with wasps, hornets, jumper ants, and honey bees. However, for fire ants, whole-body extract is still used in the US, and the latter practice has not yet been subjected to a randomized controlled efficacy trial. In VIT, gradually increasing doses of insect venom are administered to induce immunological tolerance, typically by subcutaneous injection at an interval of several weeks for up to 5 years. Extrapolating from randomized controlled trial evidence in relation to hay fever, a treatment course of 3 years is recommended, although longer courses are recommended in some settings. Immunotherapy works through complex immunological mechanisms. The initial mechanism of action is a mast cell and basophil desensitization, followed by changes in T-cells (including the formation of T regulatory cells to the allergen) and finally an alteration in B-cell, IgE (an initial rise, followed by a reduction over several months), mast cell, basophil, and eosinophil responses to the allergen.(Ludman *et.al.*, 2015)

5.8.1.VIT treatment protocols :

VIT is commercially available for honeybee, paper wasp, and yellow jacket ("European") wasps since these are the commonest causes of venom anaphylaxis worldwide. To our knowledge, immunotherapy products for ant allergy are not currently commercially available. This review will therefore focus on wasp and honeybee VIT using extracted venom. At present, the treatment offered for venom allergy is largely via subcutaneous immunotherapy (SCIT). Treatment regimes are diverse and the populations they have been tested on vary. This makes comparison between schedules difficult. Improvement of honeybee immunotherapy efficacy may be possible by increasing the quantities of major determinants such as Api m 3 and 10 in VIT preparation, or tailoring the allergenic component mix according to individual patient sensitization pattern. This could be done by improving the method of generating the venom preparation, spiking the venom with recombinant allergens, or tailoring the immunotherapy for different patients with a range of component allergens relevant for that patient.(Ludman *et.al.*, 2015)

VIT starting doses are often around 0.0001 μg per injection and rise to a maintenance does of 100 μg (approximately two bee stings or 30 wasp stings). In children, data from a small study suggest that a lower 50 μg maintenance dose provides effective protection from SRs with potentially improved safety profile. Longer induction-phase treatments can be done as an outpatient; however, for rush therapy, hospital admission is advisable. Although the safety profile of semi-rush and ultrarush VIT up-dosing protocols is good, in general, accelerated up-dosing immunotherapy protocols are associated with increased risk of systemic allergic reaction to VIT. The maintenance dose interval has historically been set at 1 month but studies have shown that intervals of up to 3–4 months retain their efficacy. In patients who experience SRs to stings during the traditional regime induction, accelerated induction protocols have been successfully used. If a patient experiences a SR during maintenance VIT then a larger dose of 200 μg can be given, although switching to a lower maintenance dose for a prolonged period may be needed first.(Ludman *et.al.*, 2015)

Venom immunotherapy (VIT) is the only effective treatment for prevention of further anaphylactic reactions to bee and wasp stings in allergic individuals. A previous national survey carried out in 2006/2007 revealed significant heterogeneity in UK practice. The British Society for Allergy and Clinical Immunology (BSACI) guidelines for the diagnosis and management of hymenoptera venom (HV) allergy were subsequently published in 2011 This repeat survey was carried out to assess whether publication of BSACI guidelines helped improve the diagnosis and management of HV allergy in the UK National Health Service (NHS). (Diwakar *et.al.*, 2016)

The diagnosis of erucism is straight forward because the victim usually brings the caterpillar. The best method to control the pain is nerve block anesthesia with 2% lidocaine, but in children (the majority of victims), the recommendation is to apply topical commercial anesthetic creams with 0.25% lidocaine and 0.25% prilocaine. Additional treatments include the application of cold compresses, oral antihistamines, and topical corticosteroids, which reduce local inflammation, but not the pain.(Haddad, 2014)

CHAPTER SIX

Discussion

6.0.Discussion :

According to Shrivastava (1993) insect venoms are introduced into the body of man and animals in one of the following three ways :

i. by the bite
ii. by the sting and
iii. by the contact.

There are three categories of insects that are poisons namely stinging, biting and vesicating. In bees, wasps and ants the ovipositor was modified to function as stinging apparatus.In bees, stinging apparatus has 3 major components, a piercing shaft or dart composing a pair of stylets and a pair of lancets, and distally barbed structure, two pairs of layers to which the y-shaped arms of the shaft are attached and worked by powerful muscles and a pair of glands, a long and slender acid gland opening on top of a large poison sac into poison gland. A small alkaline poison gland is located at the base of the poison sac which also opens into poison duct. Due to the barbed tips of the piercing shaft, the sting gets stuck into the wound and then detached, continuing to operate even in the detached condition. Wasps, ants and bees showed sting. In most of the insects poison glands were modified from accessory glands.

According to Shrivastava (1993) bees were divided into two groups namely, those that sting to kill and those that sting to paralyze. The former possess two poison glands, the acidic and alkaline glands. The poison of this group was the combination of the acid and alkaline fluids which resulted in death or caused extreme pain and reactions in man. In bee venom the chief components were a protein called melittin that has powerful haemolytic allergic actions in humans. The enzymes such as lecithinase (Phospholipase-A) and hyaluronidase have also played a very important role in poisoning reactions. Lecithinase inhibited lactic dehydronages and citric acid cycle substrates leading to intense pain in the victim while, the enzyme hyaluronidase helped to spread other components to the tissues. According to Strother (1985) Hymenopterous insects like ants, bees, hornets and yellow jackets caused more severe allergic reactions than other insects. The imported fire ant inflicted a very painful sting resulting in postulation at the sting site.

CHAPTER SEVEN

Summary and conclusion

7.0. Summary and conclusion :

Most insects do not usually attack humans unless they are provoked. Many bites and stings are defensive. Insects sting to protect their hives or nests or when incidentally touched or disturbed (so hives and nests should not be disturbed or approached). A sting or bite injects venom composed of proteins and other substances that may trigger an allergic reaction in the victim. The sting also causes redness and swelling at the site of the sting.(Bees, wasps, hornets, yellow jackets, and fire ants are members of the Hymenoptera family). Bites or stings from these species may cause serious reactions in people who are allergic to them. Death from bee stings is 3 to 4 times more common than death from snake bites.

- When a bee stings, it loses the entire injection apparatus (stinger) and actually dies in the process.
- A wasp can inflict multiple stings because it does not lose its injection apparatus after it stings.
- Fire ants inject their venom by using their mandibles (the biting parts of their jaw) and rotating their bodies. They may inject venom many times.
- Puss caterpillars (Megalopyge opercularis or asp) have hollow "hairs" or spines (setae) that break when touched and toxin is injected into the skin.
- In contrast, bites from mosquitoes are not defensive; mosquitoes are looking to get blood for a meal.

Typically, most mosquitoes do not cause significant illnesses or allergic reactions unless they convey "vectors," or pathogenic microorganisms that actually live within the mosquitoes. For instance:

- Malaria is caused by an organism that spends part of its life cycle in a particular species of mosquitoes.
- West nile virus is another disease spread by a mosquito. Various mosquitoes spread other viral diseases such as
- Equine encephalitis;
- Zika virus (suspected of causing microcephaly);
- Dengue; and
- Yellow fever to humans and other animals.

Other types of insects or bugs that bite for a blood meal and diseases that are possibly transmitted are as follows:

- Lice bites can transmit epidemic relapsing fever, caused by spirochetes (bacteria).
- Leishmaniasis, caused by the protozoan *Leishmania*, is carried by a sand fly bite.
- Sleeping sickness in humans and a group of cattle diseases that are widespread in Africa, and known as, are caused by protozoan trypanosomes transmitted by the bites of tsetse flies.
- Bacteria-caused diseases tularemia can be spread by deer fly bites, the bubonic plague by fleas, and the epidemic typhus rickettsia by lice.
- Ticks (arachnids) can transmit Lyme disease and several other illnesses through their bites; ticks bite so they can obtain a blood meal.

- Other arachnids (bugs) such as chiggers, bedbugs, and mites typically cause self-limited localized itchiness and occasional swelling.
- Serious bites from spiders (arachnids), which are not insects, can be from the black widow or brown recluse spiders; the spiders bite usually as a defense mechanism.

Other insects and bugs can transmit diseases by simply transferring pathogens like *Salmonella spp* by contact. For example, in unsanitary conditions, the common housefly can play an incidental role in the spread of human intestinal infections (such as typhoid, bacillary and amebic dysentery) by contamination of human food as it lands and "walks" over foods after previously "walking" on contaminated items like feces.Accidents caused by encounters with venomous animals and insects are some of the most neglected health threats affecting predominately poor rural commodities.

International attention and response is needed to ameliorate this problem. Although travelers rarely face life-threatening accidents, morbidity- particularly caused by venomous marine animals is the importance in this group. Given the current level of international mobility of individuals, clinicians and travel clinics need to be able to give advice on the prevention, first aid and clinicl management of envenoming. In patients with hymenoptera allergy, such as the patient described in the vignette, venom immunotherapy is the standard of treatment and can prevent life-threatening anaphylactic reactions. Epinephrine is the mainstay of treatment for patient who have a severe reactions to a hymenoptera sting, patient with a history of systemic allergic reaction should be instructed regarding the need to carry an epinephrine auto injector and to use it as needed, including possible more than one injection per reaction (Casale *et.al.*, 2014)

Hence the poisonous insects are harmful to humans and other living being, we should have knowledge on insect bites and aware to avoid or overcome from insect poisoning in future.

References

Abrishami, M.A., G.K. Boyd and G.A Settipane. 1971. Prevalence of bee sting allergy in 2,010 Girl Scouts. *Acta AUergol*; **26**: 117—120.

Alvarez, F.J. 2014. The effect of chitin size, shape, source and purification method on immune recognition. *Molecules*, 19**(4)**: 4433-4451.

Anonymous. 1797. Natural History of the Rarer Lepidopterous Insects of Georgia. Vol. 1. Bensley, London. 100 pp.

Anonymous. 1961. Wild Silkmoths of the United States: Saturniinae. Experimental Studies and Observations of Natural Living Habits and Relationships. 1961. Collins Radio Company. Cedar Rapids, Iowa. 138 pp.

Anonymous. 1981. Structures, properties, and functions of the stings of honey bees https://www.ncbi.nlm.nih.gov. NCBI. PubMed Central (PMC).

Anonymous. 1987. Saturniidae (Bombycoidea). *In* Stehr FW. (ed.). Immature Insects. Kendall/Hunt. Dubuque, Iowa. pp. 513-521.

Anonymous. 1990. Spiders and their kin. Golden press, New York.

Anonymous. 1993. Horse-flies, deer-flies and clegs (Tabanidae). In Lane, R.P. Crosskey, R.W. Medical Insects and Arachnids. Springer. pp. 310–332.

Anonymous. 1993. Physician"s Guide to Arthropods of medical importance. CRC press, Boca Raton, FL.

Anonymous. 1993. Venomous Arthropods and Treatments of their venoms in A text book of Applied Entomology. Pp-262-269.

Anonymous. 1999. A field guide to the spiders and scorpions of Texas. Gulf publishing, Houston, TX.

Anonymous. 1999. Venomous Terrestrial Animals of Texas. Safety and Environment Awareness committee, Equister Chemical, LP. Pp. 4-15.

Anonymous. 2009. Venomous and poisonous arthropods: identification,clinical scielo.br.www.scielo.br/scielo.php?script=sci_arttext&pid=S0037- 86822015000600650.

Anonymous. 2012. A striking aberrant *Automeris io*. Association for Tropical Lepidoptera Notes. Gainesville, Florida. pp. 4.

Anonymous. 2012. Peterson Field Guide to Moths of Northeastern North America. Houghton Mifflin. New York, N. Y. 611 pp.

Anonymous. 2014. *Seizure and Ischemic Attack Following Bee Sting JournalAgent*. https://www.journalagent.com/z4/download_fulltext.asp?pdir=tjn&ppdf=2.

Archer, M.E. 1998. Taxonomy, distribution and nesting biology of Vespa orientalis L.(Hymenoptera Vespidae. *Entomologist's Monthly Magazine*. **138**: 45–51.

Arnaud, P.H. 1978. A Host-Parasite Catalog of North American Tachinidae (Diptera). United States Department of Agriculture Miscellaneous Publication. Washington, D.C.

Axtell, R.C., T.D. Edwards and J.C. Dukes. 1975. Rigid canopy trap for Tabanidae (Diptera). Journal of the Georgia Entomological Society. 10 **(1)**: 64–67.

Battisti, A, G. Holm, B. Fagrell, S. Larsson. 2011. Urticating hairs in arthropods: their nature and medical significance. *Annual Review of Entomology*,56: 203-220.

Bhoje, P.M., S.H. Kurane, A.S. Desai and T.V. Sathe. 2014. Biodiversity of Ants (Hymenoptera:

Bishopp, F.C. 1923. The puss caterpillar and the effects of its sting on man. United States Department of Agriculture. *Department Circular*. **288**. Pp.14.

Blest, A.D. 1957. The function of eyespot patterns in the Lepidoptera. *Behaviour,* 11**(2/3)**: 209-255.

Brodie, E.D. 1989. Poisonous Insects Birmingham, Alabama (AL) - Children's of Alabama. www.childrensal.org. Child Safety Institute. Poison Control Center.

Brown., Eryn. 2012. Brown widow spiders taking over in Southern California. Science Now *Los Angeles Times*.

Cashin Garbutt., B.A. Hons. 2013. Complications of insect bites - News Medical. https://www.news medical.net/health/Complications-of-insect-bites.aspx

Chrysis shanghaiensis Smith. 2016. A Parasite of Parasa lepida Cr. Proceedings of the Royal Entomological Society of London. Series A, General Entomology. **12**: 11.

Da Silva, C.A., C. Chalouni, A. Williams, D. Hartl, C.G. Lee, J.A, Elias. 2009. Chitin is a size-dependent regulator of macrophage TNF and IL-10 production. *Journal of Immunology* ,182**(6)**: 3573-3582.

Daly, Frank, Hill, E.Robert, Bogdan, M. Gregory, Dart, C. Richard, Dart, C. Richard. 2001. Neutralization of Latrodectus mactans and L. hesperus Venom by Redback Spider (L.hasseltii) antivenom. Clinical Toxicology. 39 **(2)**: 119–23.

David, B.K. 2011. Stinging insect hypersensitivity. *Annals of Allergy & Asthma*.(16).

Davidson, S.A, S.A. Norton, M.C. Carder, M. Debboun. 2009. Outbreak of dermatitis linearis caused by Paederus ilsae and Paederus iliensis (Coleoptera: Staphylinidae) at a military base in Iraq. U.S. Army Medical Department Journal: 6–15.

Davidson,F.F. 1967. Biology of laboratory-reared *Megalopyge opercularis* Sm. & Abb.Morphology and histology of the stinging mechanism. *Texas Journal of Science*. **19**: 258- 274.

Diaz, J.H. 2005. The evolving global epidemiology, syndromic classification, management, and prevention of caterpillar envenoming. *American Journal of Tropical Medicine and Hygiene*, 72**(3)**: 347-357.

Dvorak, Libor. 2006. Oriental Hornet Vespa orientalis Linnaeus, 1771 found in Mexico. *Entomological Problems*. **36**: 80.

Eagleman, D.M. 2008. Envenomation by the asp caterpillar (*Megalopyge opercularis*). *Clinical Toxicology*. **46**: 201-205.

Ebeling, W. 1975. Urban Entomology. Oakland*: Univ. Calif. Agric. Nat. Sci.*

Ellis, A. K. and J. H. Day. 2003. Diagnosis and management of anaphylaxis. *Canadian Medical*

Epstein, M.E. 1996. Revision and phylogeny of the limacodid-group families, with evolutionary studies on slug caterpillars (Lepidoptera: Zygaenoidea). *Smithsonian Contributions to Zoology*. **582:**102.

Everson, G.W, J.B, Chapin, S.A. Normann. 1990. Caterpillar envenomations: a prospective study of 112 cases. *Veterinary and Human Toxicology*, 32: 114-119.

Floater, G.J. 1998. Tuff scales and egg protection in Ochrogaster lunifer Herrichschatter (Lepidoptera : Thaumetopoeidea). *Australian J. Ent*., **37**, 34-39. Formicidae) of Amba reserve Forest of Western Ghats, Maharashtra. *Global J. Res. Analysis*, 3**(7)**: 284-287.

Frank, J.H, K. Kanamitsu. 1987. Paederus, sensu lato (Coleoptera: Staphylinidae): natural history and medical importance. Journal of Medical Entomology. 24 **(2)**: 155–91.

Frank, J.H. (1988). Paederus, sensu lato (Coleoptera: Staphylinidae): An index and review of the taxa. Insecta Mundi. 2 **(2)**: 97–159.

Fred A. Lawson, *et.al.*, 1996. Insects affecting man - Wyoming Extension. uwyoextension.org/psep/wp-content/uploads/2012/09/MP-21.pdf.

Gal Haspel. 2003. Parasitoid wasp affects metabolism of cockroach host. *The Gefen Lab*. www.gefenlab.com/uploads/2/0/9/5/20958696/2005_haspel_et_al.pdf.

Geoffrey Ingersoll. 2013. http://www.businessinsider.in/This-Is-What-The-Sting-From-Those- Killer-Giant-Hornets-In-China-Looks-Like/articleshow/23475257.cms

Gerritsen, V.B. 2001. Princess Bala's sting. *Protein Spotlight*. **(14)**: 1–2.

Gilmer, P.M. 1925. A comparative study of the poison apparatus of certain lepidopterous larvae. *Annals of the Entomological Society of America*, 18: 203-239.

Goldman, L, F. Sawyer, A, Levine, J. Goldman, S. Goldman, J. Spinanger. 1960. Investigative studies of skin irritations from caterpillars. *Journal of Investigative Dermatology*, 34**(1)**: 67- 79.

Gordh, G, D.H. Headrick. 2001. A Dictionary of Entomology. CABI Publishing. New York. Pp. 1032.

Haddad-Jr .V, J.L.C. Cardoso, R.C. Moraes. 2002. Skin lesions caused by stink bugs (Insecta:Hemiptera: Pentatomidae). *Wild Environ Med*. **13**:48-50.

Haddad-Jr V, Lastória JC. Envenomation by caterpillars (erucism): proposal for simple pain relief treatment. J Venom Anim Toxins Incl Trop Dis 2014; 20:21.

Haddad-Jr. V. 2014. Sign of the kiss in dermatitis caused by vesicant beetles (*Paederus* sp. or " potós"). *An Bras Dermatol.* **89**: 996-997.

Hamilton, W. D. 1964. The genetical evolution of social behaviour, I & II. *Journal of Theoretical Biology*. 7 **(1)**: 1–52.

Hampson, G. F. 1892. The Fauna of British India Including Ceylon and Burma-Moths.

Herzig. V, R. John Ward, W. Ferreira dos Santos. 2002. Intersexual variations in the venom of the Brazilian armed spider Phoneutria nigriventer. Toxicon. 40 **(10)**:1399–406.

Hessel, S.A. 1964. A bilateral gynandromorph of *Automeris io* (Saturniidae) taken at mercury vapor light in Connecticut. *Journal of the Lepidopterists' Society,* 18: 27-31.

Hossler, E.W, D.M. Elston, D.L. Wagner. 2008. What's eating you? Io moth (*Automeris io*).*Cutis,* 82: 21-24.

Hughes, G, T. Rosen. 1980. *Automeris io* (caterpillar) dermatitis. *Cutis,* 26: 71-73.

Isbister G.K. and P.I. Whelan. 2000. Envenomation by the billygoat plum stinging caterpillar. *Thosea penthima. Medical J. Australia,* **173**, 654-655.

Isbister, G.K, M.R. Gray, C.R. Balit, R.J. Raven, B.J. Stokes, K. Porges, A.S. Tankel, E. Turner, J. White, M.M. Fisher. 2005. Funnel-web spider bite: A systematic review of recorded clinical cases. The Medical journal of Australia. 182 **(8)**: 407–11.

Isbister, K. Geoffrey, B. Colin, Buckley, A. Nicholas, Fatovich, M, Daniel, Pascu, Ovidiu MacDonald, P.J. Stephen, Calver, A. Leonie, Brown, G.A. Simon. 2014. Randomized Controlled Trial of Intravenous Antivenom Versus Placebo for Latrodectism: The Second Redback Antivenom Evaluation (RAVE-II) Study. Annals of Emergency Medicine. 64 **(6)**: 620–8.

Isbister, K. Geoffrey, Fan, Hui Wen. 2011. Spider bite. The Lancet. 378 **(9808)**: 2039–47.

Isbister, K. Geoffrey, Gray, R. Mike. 2004. Bites by Australian mygalomorph spiders (Araneae, Mygalomorphae), including funnel-web spiders (Atracinae) and mouse spiders(Actinopodidae: Missulena spp). Toxicon. 43 **(2)**: 133–40.

Jacobs, B. Steven. 2009. Entomological Notes: Brown Marmorated Stink Bug. Pennsylvania State University Department of Agriculture.

Jacobs, Steve. 2010. Penn State University College of Agricultural Sciences.

James M. Carpenter. 2008. Review of Hawaiian Vespidae (Hymenoptera). *Occasional Papers of the Bishop Museum.* **99**: 1–18.

Kahan, E. 1997. Toxins Defensive Compoun ds and Drugs from Insects.

Khalaf, K.T. 1974. Nonaseptic wheat germ diet for *Megalopyge opercularis.* (Lepidoptera: Megalopygidae). *Florida Entomologist.* **57**: 377-381.

Klotz, 2008 & 2010. Kissing bugs. potential disease vectors and cause of anaphylaxis. Clinical Infectious Diseases. 50 **(12)**: 1629–34.

Koehler P.G. and J.W.Diclaro. 2011. Stinging or venomous insects and related pests. *IFAS Extension University of Florida, EVY.*215.

Koehler, P.G, R.M. Pereira, J.W. Diclaro. 2016. Fleas.

Korman, S.H. 1990 .https://www.ncbi.nlm.nih.gov/pubmed/2265021.

Kowacs, P.A., J. Cardoso, M. Entres, E. Novak, L. Werneck. 2006. Fatal intracerebral hemorrhage secondary to Lonomia obliqua caterpillar envenoming: case report. Arquivos de Neuro- Psiquiatria. 64 **(4)**: 1030–2.

Laurance, Jeremy 2010. The rural flies with a taste for city flesh. The Independent. London.28.

Lefroy, M.H., and F.M. Howlett. 1909. Indian Insects Life . A manual of the insects of the plains (Tropical India). *Today & Tomorrow's Print & Publi. New Delhi.* Pp.521-523.

Mallakh, R.S., M.S. Baumgartner, N. Fares. 1986. Sting of the puss caterpillar, *Megalopyge opercularis* (Lepidoptera: Megalopygidae).*The Journal of the Florida Medical Association.* **73**: 521-525.

Manley, T.R. 1971. Two mosaic gynandromorphs of *Automeris io* (Saturniidae). *Journal of the Lepidopterists Society*, 25: 234-238.

Menke, A.S. 1960. A taxonomic study of the genus Abedus Stål (Hemiptera,Belostomatidae). University of California Publications in Entomology. 16 **(8)**: 393–440.

Murphy, S.M, S.M. Leahy, L.S. Williams, J.T. Lill. 2010. Stinging spines protect slug caterpillars (Limacodidae) from multiple generalist predators. *Behavioral Ecology,* 21:153-160.

National Jewish Health, 2005. Allergies to Insect Venom - National Jewish Health. https://www.nationaljewish.org/NJH/media/pdf/pdf-MF-Allergies- to -Venom.pdf

Pawara, R. H ., N.G Patel, J.V. Pawara, P.J. Gavit and S.S. Ishi. 2014. Beetles of jalgaon district of Maharashtra, India. *Biolife*, 2**(3)**:970-973.

Perez Goodwyn, P. J. 2006. Taxonomic revision of the subfamily Lethocerinae Lauck & Menke (Heteroptera: Belostomatidae). Stuttgarter Beiträge zur Naturkunde, Serie A (Biologie). **695**: 1–71.

Pest Animal ControlArchived. 2008. *Bay of Plenty environment report.*

Pet Assure Corp.1996-2017.Insect Bites on Dogs: Signs, Symptoms and Treatment-Pet Assure .https://www.petassure.com/new-newsletters/insect- bites-on-dogs

Robert. 2017. 10 Most Venomous Spiders in the World - Toptenz.net. www.toptenz.net/10- venomous-spiders-world.php

Robinson, H. William. 2005. Urban Insects and Arachnids: A Handbook of Urban Entomology. Cambridge University Press. pp.51.

Roy.J.Ledbetter1985. Stinging Insects and Poisonous Spiders of Alabama.www.aces.edu/pubs/docs/A/ANR-0382/ANR-0382.pdf

Sathe, T.V. 2007. Biodiversity of wild silk months from Western Maharashtra, India. *Bull. Ind. Acad. Seri,* 2**(1)**:21-24.

Sathe, T.V. 2014. Ecology, epidemiology and control of Sand flies from Kolhapur region, India. *Int. J. Pharma. Bio.Sci.* 5 **(4)**: 1037- 145..

Sathe, T.V. 2014. Harmful Syntomids (Syntomidae : Lepidoptera) of agro and forest crop plants from Western Maharashtra, India. *Cib. Tech. J. Zool,* 3**(3)**:22-25.

Sathe, T.V. 2015. Insects for human diet from Kolhapur region, India. *Int. J. Pharma. Bio.Sci.*6**(1)** :519-527.

Sathe, T.V., and Jadav Divya. 2014. Ecology and control of eye flies *Siphunculina spp.* (Chloropidae:Diptera). *Int. J. Pharma. Bio.Sci*,5**(4)**: 214-220.

Scott R. Craven. 2010. Outdoor Hazards in Wisconsin - Shawano County - UW Extension.https://shawano.uwex.edu/files/2010/05/Outdoor-Hazards-in-WI.pdf

Settipane, G.A, G.J. Newstead, G.K. Boyd. 1972. Frequency of Hymenoptera allergy in an atopic and normal population. *J Allergy Chn Immunol*, **50**: 146-150.

Sian.W.Ludman. 2015. Stinging insect allergy: current perspectives on venomimmunotherapy.https://www.ncbi.nlm.nih.gov/pmc/articles/PMC4517515.

Southcott, R.V. 1978. Lepidopterism in the Australian region. *Records of the Adelaide Childrens Hospital*, **2:** 87-173.

Southcott, R.V. 1987. Moths and butterflies in Toxic plants and animals, A gunde for Australia queensland Museum.

Starr, Christoper. 1987. Nest-site Preferences of the Giant Honey Bee, Apis dorsata (Hymeoptera:Apidae), in Borneo. Pan-Pacific Entomologist **(63)**: 37–42.

Strother, G.R. 1985. Stinging insects and poisonous spiders of Alabama. Pest management Fact sheet. *Circular ANR*-382:47.

Syed, Z., Leal, W. S. 2009. Acute olfactory response of Culex mosquitoes to a human- and bird- derived attractant. Proceedings of the National Academy of Sciences. 106 **(44)**.

The EAACI Food Allergy and Anaphylaxis Guidelines Group. 2014. European Academy of Allergy and Clinical Immunology.69 **(8)**.

Theodore M. Freeman, M.D. 2013. Hypersensitivity to Hymenoptera Stings. *The new england journal of medicine*,351.

Thomas B. Casale, M.D., and A. Wesley Burks, M.D. 2014. Hymenoptera-Sting Hypersensitivity.*The new england journal of medicine*. 370.

Walker, A.R. 1994. Arthropods of Humans and Domestic Animals: A Guide to Preliminary Identification. Springer Science & Business Media. pp. 78–79.

Walker, John Lewis 2002. Shakespeare and the Classical Tradition: *An Annotated Bibliography*. pp. 363.

Wandering Spiders of the Amazon . 2013. Phoneutria - introduction. Staatliches Museum für Naturkunde Karlsruhe (State Museum of Natural History Karlsruhe).

Whelan, P.I. 2010. Stinging and itchy caterpillars in top end of the NT. Department of Health and families.

White, 2013. The Sydney Funnel-Web Spider Australian Associated Press. Australia's 'biggest ever' antivenom dose saves boy bitten by funnel web spider | Environment. The Guardian. pp. 182.

Wiener, Saul . 1956. The Australian Red Back Spider (Latrodectus Hasseltii):II. Effect of Temperature on the Toxicity of Venom. The Medical Journal of Australia. **43**: 331–34.

9 798889 866695

Printed by Libri Plureos GmbH in Hamburg,
Germany